Elite • 224

Israeli Paratroopers 1954–2016

DAVID CAMPBELL

ILLUSTRATED BY PETER DENNIS
Series editor Martin Windrow

OSPREY
Bloomsbury Publishing Plc
PO Box 883, Oxford, OX1 9PL, UK
1385 Broadway, 5th Floor, New York, NY 10018, USA
E-mail: info@ospreypublishing.com
www.ospreypublishing.com

OSPREY is a trademark of Osprey Publishing Ltd

First published in Great Britain in 2018

A catalogue record for this book is available from the British Library

ISBN: PB 9781472827715; eBook 9781472827708; ePDF 9781472827692; XML 9781472827685

18 19 20 21 22   10 9 8 7 6 5 4 3 2 1

Editor: Martin Windrow
Index by Fionbar Lyons
Typeset by PDQ Digital Media Solutions, Bungay, UK
Printed in China through World Print Ltd

Osprey Publishing supports the Woodland Trust, the UK's leading woodland conservation charity. Between 2014 and 2018 our donations are being spent on their Centenary Woods project in the UK.

To find out more about our authors and books, visit **www.ospreypublishing.com**. Here you will find extracts, author interviews, details of forthcoming events, and the option to sign up for our newsletter.

DEDICATION

To Alistair McLean. Bàs no Beatha, indeed.

ACKNOWLEDGEMENTS

Thanks are due to Ilana Dayan and the Israeli Government Press Office (http://gpophoto.gov.il/haetonot) for permission to use David Rubringer's iconic image of the three paratroopers at the Western Wall, and for its enlightened approach to the sharing and distribution of images from its archive; these are credited to (GPO) in the relevant captions.
Also, to Graham Campbell for facilitating much-needed digital back-up services; to Geoff Banks, for never failing to fail to live up to even the most modest of expectations; to Nick Reynolds, for his help in getting the project started and for his advice along the way; and to Martin Windrow, for his encouragement, advice and patience throughout the whole process.

EDITOR'S NOTE

Hebrew script has only upper-case characters. To avoid large numbers of words in capital letters, this text instead uses capitalized italics for Hebrew titles of, e.g., ranks, units and operations.

ARTIST'S NOTE

Reader may care to note that the original paintings from which the colour plates in this book were prepared are available for private sale. All reproduction copyright whatsoever is retained by the publisher. All enquiries should be addressed to:

Peter Dennis, 'Fieldhead', The Park, Mansfield, Nottinghamshire, NG18 2AT, UK

The publishers regret that they can enter into no correspondence upon this matter.

TITLE PAGE PHOTO: Paratroopers disembarking from M3 half-tracks during spring manoeuvres in 1970. Israeli armoured and infantry doctrine developed in a haphazard fashion, governed by practical experience and the capabilities of the available equipment. The paratroopers' role as an elite infantry brigade meant that they often operated as mechanized infantry like the IDF's Golani, Givati and (from 1982) Nahal brigades. (Moshe Milner, GPO)

Table of Israel Defense Forces ranks

(NATO)	US Army	IDF (& abbreviation)
(OF-10)	General of the Army	*Rav aluf*[1] *(Ra'al)*
(OF-9)	General	–
(OF-8)	Lieutenant-General	–
(OF-7)	Major-General	*Aluf*
(OF-6)	Brigadier-General	*Tat aluf (Ta'al)*
(OF-5)	Colonel	*Aluf mishne (Alam)*
(OF-4)	Lieutenant-Colonel	*Sgan aluf (Sa'al)*
(OF-3)	Major	*Rav seren (Rasan)*
(OF-2)	Captain	*Seren*
(OF-1)	1st Lieutenant	*Segen*[2]
(OF-1)	2nd Lieutenant	*Segen mishne*
–	–	*Katzín akademai bakhír (Ka'ab)*[3]
–	–	*Katzín miktsoí akademai (Kama)*[4]
(OR-9)	Chief Warrant Officer	*Rav nagad (Ranag)*[5]
(OR-9)	Warrant Officer	*Rav nagad mishne (Ranam)*[6]
(OR-9)	Command Sergeant-Major	*Rav samal bakhír (Rasab)*
(OR-8)	Sergeant-Major	*Rav samal mitkadem (Rasam)*
(OR-8)	Master Sergeant	*Rav samal rishon (Rasar)*
(OR-7)	Sergeant First Class	*Rav samal (Rasal)*
(OR-6)	Staff Sergeant	*Samal rishon (Samar)*
(OR-5)	Sergeant	*Samal*
(OR-4)	Corporal	*Rav Turai (Rabat)*
(OR-2)	Private	*Turai*

Notes:

1. *Rav aluf* is sometimes translated as 'lieutenant-general', but is a rank held only by the IDF's Chief of General Staff, the *Ramatkal* (an abbreviation of *Rosh HaMateh HaKlali*, 'Chief of the General Staff')

2. The rank of *Segen* (literally 'deputy') originated in 1951; from 1948 to 1951 it was *Segen rishon* ('first deputy')

3. 'Senior Academic Officer': A professional officer (medical service, dental medical service, veterinary service, officer of justice, officer of religion) of the first class in the reserve, equivalent to brevet captain

4. 'Professional Academic Officer' (see branches above) of the second class in the reserve, equivalent to brevet 1st lieutenant

5. Since 1993

6. Since 2011

CONTENTS

ISRAELI PARATROOPERS 1954–2016

INTRODUCTION

Paratroopers have existed in one form or another since the inception of the state of Israel itself, the first group of them being assembled during the 1948 War of Independence. The evolution from that small force, less than a company in size, to the present establishment of one regular and four reserve

paratroop brigades, has matched – even exceeded – the growth of the rest of the Israel Defense Forces (IDF). The relationship between the nation and its armed forces has traditionally been exceptionally strong, in part due to the nature of the 'founding struggle' of 1948–49 and the myths that naturally accompanied such an endeavour, and in part to the solidarity that comes with the near universal nature of service by Israeli citizens within those armed forces. It is enhanced by the shared sense of an ever-present existential threat, since during its first decades of national existence Israel was surrounded by enemies on all sides.

The initial development of parachute forces in the IDF was haphazard and not overly promising. They shared many of the problems endemic within the newly formed army, including shortages of arms, equipment and vehicles at every level. There were also inherent difficulties in incorporating the newly raised conscript soldiers into a military system that had succeeded in the past due to its reliance upon the commitment of volunteers who brought individual flair, courage and initiative to the fight. Added to this was the unsettling reality

The very different appearance of *Tzanhanim* in the field, here photographed taking a brief rest during an exercise on the Golan Heights. Note the use of the *Mitznefet* or 'clown hat', the large, loose cloth that disguises the outline of helmets, and also of 'fleeces'. These jackets (either issued or privately purchased) are popular when conducting operations in the elevated and chilly terrain of the Golan or southern Lebanon. The soldier at left is armed with an M4 fitted with an ACOG sight, bipod, and 'jungle-style' magazine coupler. (Photo by David Silverman/Getty Images)

of the new state's porous borders, the source of repeated incursions by a mix of Palestinian refugees, common bandits, and groups of *fedayeen* intent on causing mayhem. The various elements of the IDF tasked with interdicting such attacks were often unsuccessful, and their attempts at reprisal were often not much better.

The merging in 1954 of the first paratroop unit, Battalion 890, with the guerrillas of Unit 101, was the catalyst for the development of a far more effective force. In its ranks the élan of the War of Independence was seen once again; the soldiers took their roles seriously, quickly becoming a self-selecting aggressive elite. New small-unit tactics were developed, to notable effect in raids and counter-insurgency actions, which set a standard for the rest of the IDF to follow. Expansion to a brigade-size force was accomplished just before the Suez Crisis gave the paratroopers the opportunity to demonstrate their value (and a few of their lesser-noticed shortcomings) in the face of the Egyptian enemy. The success of their endeavours in 1956 cemented their place at the heart of the IDF.

In the succeeding years the force would expand, adding new reserve brigades to its roster, all of which would see much action in the wars to come, but it is arguable that it was through example and leadership that the paratroopers would make their most important impact. Many officers who had come up through the paratroop battalions went on to serve in other infantry and armoured brigades, taking with them the ethos that they had absorbed, and inculcating their new commands with the ideas and practices that had formed their military education. Individual forces such as the Golani Brigade were made into far more effective fighting units through such a process, and the effects of the 'paratrooper ethos' were further diversified and reinforced by the fact that of the IDF's 21 Chiefs of the General Staff, no fewer than eight had their start in a paratroop battalion.

The paratroopers have not been immune to the wider problems looming over the IDF in recent decades. These include the gradual reduction in the proportion of Israelis who serve in their armed forces, thus potentially weakening the traditionally strong bond between those forces and the

OPPOSITE
An honour guard of 35 Paratroopers Brigade at the Yad Vashem institute in Jerusalem on Holocaust Martyrs' and Heroes' Remembrance Day, 11 April 2012. They wear *Madei-A* ('Class A') uniform, the most notable feature of which is the paratrooper's '*Yarkit*', a four-pocket jacket with a narrow integral cloth belt, which is essentially unchanged since its introduction at the time of the brigade's formation. Note how the web belt is worn below the flaps of the skirt pockets; this is a fashion dating from 1950, shortly after the formation of Paratroopers Battalion 890. **Note that uniforms, insignia, weapons & equipment are described mainly in the colour-plate commentaries spaced throughout the text.** (GPO)

state; and the increase in domestic scrutiny and criticism that have grown apace with the army's evolution away from the conventional high-intensity warfare of the 1960s and '70s to more complex asymmetric engagements with militias, irregular forces and discontented civilian populations. The general and often violent instability dogging several of the states surrounding Israel – not to mention increasing shifts in the geopolitical systems that had previously locked the region into a stagnant but more or less stable rictus for the past 40 years – will make more demands on the IDF's capacity to anticipate a broad range of threats, demanding greater planning and flexibility in response. Whatever the future holds, the men and women of the regular and reserve paratroop brigades are certain to play their part in it.

ORIGINS

Battalion 890

The founder and first commander of Israeli parachute troops was Maj Yoel Palgi, a parachutist from the Yishuv (the Jewish residents of Palestine during the Mandate) and member of the *Palmach*, who had operated in Yugoslavia and his native Hungary during World War II. Tasked with developing an airborne commando unit for the *Haganah* ('The Defence', the precursor

A **1948–1955**

(1) Commando, Unit 101, 1953

There was no set uniform for the men of Ariel Sharon's Unit 101, with a variety of military and civilian clothing being worn according to personal choice or the nature of a mission. This commando wears a newly imported French stitched-fabric bush hat, a rough linen dust-scarf, a 37 Pattern British battledress blouse adorned with the Israeli parachute 'wings' badge, and a pair of domestically produced khaki trousers over British 'ammunition boots'. His British 37 Ptn web belt supports a locally-made 5-cell canvas magazine pouch (probably derived from the US 30-round magazine pouch for the Thompson M1A1), and he is armed with an MP40 sub-machine gun. At this date many weapons came from British stocks left over from the Mandate, but these were supplemented with other wartime types acquired from e.g. Czechoslovakia and France, including large numbers of Mauser Kar 98K rifles and MG34 machine guns.

(2) Paratrooper, Battalion 890, 1951

This member of the first regular airborne unit wears a locally-made khaki shirt and trousers derived from British 'khaki drill' patterns, with British boots and web anklets. British 37 Ptn webbing was common, either surplus or locally-made copies. His weapon is a second-pattern Dror ('Liberty') light machine gun, the result of one of the first attempts to establish an arms industry within Israel. At this date the nascent IDF was juggling a mix of war-surplus weapons (including the 7.92x57mm MG34, the .Browning .30cal M1919A4 and the .303in Bren, among others); the calibres were inconsistent, and the supplies of guns, ammunition and spare parts were unreliable. These problems prompted an attempt to develop a domestically produced weapon; the Dror was derived from the American M1944 Johnson LMG, for which plans and machinery were smuggled out to Israel in the late 1940s. The first pattern, made in very limited numbers, was chambered for .303in British (of which large stocks were held), but the

rimmed cartridge caused too many problems, so a second pattern was developed around the 7.92x57mm Mauser cartridge, fed by modified 20-round BAR magazines. The Dror's rushed development resulted in a temperamental weapon, both unpleasant to fire and vulnerable to dirt. It is unlikely that the gun ever saw much use in combat, being quickly relegated to the training role.

(3) Lieutenant Meir Har-Zion, Battalion 890 reconnaissance company, 1955

One of the most famous soldiers of the early IDF, Meir Har-Zion was an influential member of Unit 101; commissioned in the field (very unusually), he came to rival Ariel Sharon in his contribution to the unit's capabilities. Absorbed into the paratroopers after the disbandment of Unit 101, he was the first commander of the battalion's reconnaissance company, eventually developing it (with fellow officer Micha Ben-Ari) into a highly effective element that proved its worth in dozens of engagements. He was involved in several high-profile retaliatory operations, including *Kinneret* (Operation *Olive Leaves*) on 11 December 1955. He took part in the jump on the Mitla Pass in the 1956 Suez War/Sinai Campaign, and in Operation *Thunderbolt* on 11 September 1956, during which he was severely wounded. Invalided out of the IDF, he nevertheless returned to fight in the Six-Day War battle for Jerusalem, and again on the Golan Heights in the Yom Kippur War. Despite his impressive career and undoubted leadership qualities he was a controversial figure, not least for a personal retaliation raid into Jordan while on leave. Here, he is shown leading a squad on a night patrol. The pose obscures the new olive-coloured paratrooper's jacket or *Yarkit* and trousers; the blouse was distinguishable from that worn by other units by its extra length, four pockets and integral belt (compare with photo on page 4). He wears the tall reddish-brown jump boots that would, like the red beret, quickly become an iconic element of every paratrooper's uniform. His webbing is Israeli-made, and he too carries an MP40.

A portrait of a Haganah soldier armed with a British Mk II Sten gun during the War of Independence, 1948. Uniforms, weapons and equipment were necessarily assembled more or less at random from various foreign surplus stocks, and this remained the case during the first years of the IDF's existence. Attempts to develop domestic industries that would allow Israel a degree of self-sufficiency were begun even before the formal foundation of the state, but it would be years before local production met demand, especially for the more complex weapon systems and vehicles. (Zoltan Kluger, GPO)

to the IDF), Palgi managed to assemble around 50 volunteers for his nascent force (some of whom had similar wartime airborne experience in the Balkans), establishing a training base at Ramat David near Haifa on 2 September 1948.[1] The small force grew to around 100 men, but initially had no parachutes and only a single aircraft capable of dropping paratroops; around 50 of the men had been trained to jump on a course in Czechoslovakia, but in the end the unit saw no action during the War of Independence (May 1948–July 1949).

Things hardly improved after the war. Despite securing large numbers of surplus British parachutes as well as more aircraft, problems persisted with both the quality and availability of equipment, and several men were lost in a series of fatal training accidents. Many of the new intakes of conscripts (in line with the IDF's new policy of universal service) proved to be far from ideal paratrooper material. Such problems called the whole endeavour into question; disillusioned, Palgi resigned, and the unit was disbanded on 24 May 1949. Even so, the idea of parachute infantry remained attractive to some on the General Staff, and later that same year Yehuda Harari was appointed to re-establish it. The parachute school was moved to a new base at Tel Nof, and a new force – Battalion 890, consisting of one rifle company and one training company – was created.

The new incarnation of paratroopers took its style, as did much of the IDF, from the practice and rituals of the British forces that had until recently been the dominating presence in the Mandate. The adoption of the red beret and a distinctive four-pocket blouse (the *Yarkit*) were both inspired by the British Airborne Forces, and the reddish-brown jump boots by the US Army Airborne's 'Corcorans'. Harari's regime emphasized strict discipline, cleanliness and drill. Battalion 890 certainly looked the part, but unfortunately 'square-bashing' was not enough to turn paratroopers into effective soldiers. Engaging in cross-border patrols and reprisals was popular with Bn 890's staff (and all the other IDF units tasked with these activities); such excursions offered the chance to train units and particularly their commanders during active operations, as well as the potential intelligence that such missions could accrue. Despite this enthusiasm, the shortcomings of Bn 890 were demonstrated on several occasions during the counter-*fedayeen* reprisal operations of the early 1950s. The unit suffered from elementary failings in fieldcraft and navigation and from poor tactical training, all sometimes compounded by a lack of fighting spirit when it was time to drive an attack home.

Unit 101

The period after the end of the 1948–49 War did not see a return to peace. The foundation of the new state had caused great upheavals amongst the

---

1 During the British Mandate period which preceded Israel's independent statehood in May 1948, no overt Israeli military organization was permitted. The *Haganah* was a covert force, and the *Palmach* its 'regular' element. The *Haganah* began to operate more openly in late 1947 in the face of Arab attacks on Israeli routes of communication; by May 1948 it was nearly 29,700 strong, of which just over 3,000 were *Palmachniks*.

IDF Chief of Staff LtGen Moshe Dayan (centre), photographed on 28 October 1955 with some of the officers from Para Bn 890 who took part in the raid on the Kunteila police station in the Sinai (Operation *Egged*); most of these men would have a significant impact on the IDF. Standing, left to right: Lt Meir Har-Zion, LtCol Ariel Sharon, LtGen Dayan, Capt Danni Matt, Lt Moshe Efron, and MajGen Asaf Simchoni, assistant head of the General Staff Operations Directorate. Sitting, left to right: Capt Aharon Davidi, Lt Ya'akov Ya'akov, and Capt Rafael Eitan.

Meir Har-Zion founded his legend with Unit 101 before leading Bn 890's elite reconnaissance element. Danni Matt would go on to cement his reputation at the head of Reserve Para Bde 247 during its daring operations in the Sinai battles of the Yom Kippur War. 'Arik' Sharon would play pivotal (and controversial) roles in Israeli military and political circles over 50 years. Asaf Simchoni would be a key figure in the 1956 Suez Crisis, dying in an aircraft crash on the last day of the Sinai Campaign. Aharon Davidi would rise to the rank of brigadier before retiring in 1970; he subsequently became an academic, and also founded the IDF's Sar-El volunteer programme. 'Raful' Eitan led the Para Bde on the Gaza front during the 1967 Six-Day War, and would go on to be responsible for the fight to retain the Golan Heights in the dark days of the 1973 Yom Kippur War. Subsequently promoted to the Northern Command, he became the IDF's Chief of Staff in 1978 and played an instrumental role in launching the First Lebanon War in 1982. He retired a year later under something of a cloud, due to ambiguities over responsibility for the Sabra and Shatila massacre carried out by pro-Israeli Lebanese militiamen. (GPO)

local Palestinian population, with many fleeing the war of their own accord to seek refuge in Egypt, Gaza, Syria and the Jordanian-occupied West Bank, while others were forcibly displaced by the Israelis. Once the war had concluded many displaced Palestinians attempted to return to their old homes and villages, either temporarily or permanently. The situation was complicated both by a degree of outright banditry, as well as by the actions of the *fedayeen*, Palestinian guerrillas who made infiltrations to launch attacks on Israeli settlements and outposts. From 1951 onwards there was an increasing series of tit-for-tat actions: Palestinian incursions were followed by Israeli reprisals that were often messy and inconclusive, since the effectiveness of the IDF's infantry brigades in securing and policing the new state's borders left something to be desired.

Following a number of inconclusive or failed reprisal actions (and the political fallout that they generated), in early 1953 it was recognized that some sort of special force was required, probably around a company in size. This could operate as a series of small, highly mobile independent squads that would be able to react quickly to any infiltration, hitting back hard with accuracy and speed. To that end Unit 101 was established on 30 July 1953; the command was given to a recently retired major who was now in the reserves, Ariel Sharon – a man with a track record when it came to unconventional methods and reprisal actions. With an establishment of no more than 50 men drawn from both regulars and reservists, recruitment was informal and relied on networks of friends or former comrades. One of these was Meir Har-Zion, who would prove to be a consummate scout and the very definition of a Unit 101 soldier – intelligent, physically fit, highly aggressive, and ruthless (Morris 1997: 252). The men wore what they liked and used a variety of weapons; discipline appeared non-existent, as did distinctions of rank, and outsiders were unable to tell enlisted men from officers.

The unit quickly made its mark with highly effective reprisals, but these also proved to be bloody and controversial, with actions at the Bureij camp and the infamous assault on Qibya being among the most well-known. The latter was instigated by a grenade attack on an Israeli settlement at Yehud near the Jordanian border that killed a mother and two of her young children. Two days later, on the night of 14/15 October 1953, a combined force of about 130 men, from Unit 101 and a majority of paratroopers from Bn 890, set out on a reprisal against the village of Qibya. A Jordanian National Guard outpost was overrun, and buildings were cleared with gunfire and hand grenades before being demolished with explosives, the action costing the lives of some 50–60 civilian inhabitants. International condemnation was swift and wide-ranging, forcing Unit 101 to keep a low profile in the subsequent months. The image problem was finally resolved in January 1954 by merging 101 with Bn 890, and Sharon took command of the new unit. The former members of 101 effectively became the new battalion's *sayeret tzanhanim* (paratroop reconnaissance company), commanded by Meir Har-Zion.

B

1956 & 1967

(1) Light machine-gunner, 202 Paratroopers Brigade; Suez, 1956

Serving with the motorized relief column sent to link up with his air-dropped comrades at the Mitla Pass, this gunner has just dismounted from his half-track. He wears the British Airborne Mk II helmet with netting, standard issue for IDF paratroopers since the early 1950s, though this one lacks the black rubber band cut from a tyre inner tube to help secure the netting (a habit that would become ubiquitous throughout the IDF for all helmet types, even up to the present day). Wearing a locally-made version of the US M51 field jacket, this paratrooper carries the M1919A6, the variant of the Browning .30cal M1919A4 machine gun developed late in World War II. As a more substantial belt-fed replacement for the magazine-fed M1918A2 BAR in the infantry squad, the M1919A6 proved unsuccessful. It was too long (especially with the 1945-issued M6 flash hider attached); too heavy (at 15kg, almost double the weight of the BAR, even without ammunition); and difficult to service and use (changing barrels in the field, even after adaptations were made, was nothing like as simple as for the Bren or MG34). Gradually phased out of US use in the 1950s, many found their way to Israel. The IDF rechambered them for 7.62x51mm NATO and adapted them in other ways. Though the guns could use steel-link ammunition the IDF preferred the fabric 225/230-round belts, which fitted better into their stocks of M19A1 ammunition boxes. The weapon continued in service in various forms into the 1970s.

(2) Rifle grenadier, 55 Paratroopers Brigade (Reserve); Jerusalem, 1967

He advances with his rifle at the ready, and spare BT/AT 52 rifle grenades stuffed into his haversack for immediate use. With the British Airborne Mk II helmet he wears a French 'lizard-pattern' camouflage smock and trousers, which were common in IDF paratroop units leading up to and during the Six-Day War. This example is the TAP (*troupes aeroportées*) Mle 1947/54, though slightly differing Mle 1947/56 and Mle 58 versions were also common – there was no standardization. His webbing is the Israeli-made version common to all rifle-armed troops; derived from the US World War II pistol belt and suspenders, it has a British 37 Ptn haversack, and pouches both of 37 Ptn and of a new, smaller IDF type with deep, three-snap, hanging flaps. He is armed

with an FN FAL rifle with a 22mm rifle-grenade adapter attached. In IDF service the FAL was known as the *Rov've Mitta'enn* or *Romat* for short ('self-loading rifle'). Adopted just before the 1956 War, it would be the main battle rifle until the end of the 1973 Yom Kippur War, when it was gradually replaced with the Galil. Never popular due to its temperamental nature in sandy environments, it was also felt to be too unwieldy for infantry who were mostly transported in M3 half-tracks. The heavy-barrelled fully-automatic version, the *Makle'a Kal* or *Makleon*, was even longer and heavier. Israel was one of the countries that made significant use of rifle grenades. The BT/AT 52 (Bullet-Trap/Anti-Tank) carried a charge of RDX/TNT, and with a maximum effective range of 300m it was useful against structures and lightly armoured vehicles. Its 'bullet-trap' designation meant that it was launched using a live ball round, thus avoiding the slow and potentially dangerous substitution of a special blank round, and often a modification to the rifle's gas system, that were required for some other models.

(3) Sergeant, 80 Paratroopers Brigade (Reserve); Gaza, 1967

This Uzi-armed *Samal* is a classic example of the paratrooper commonly seen in the Six-Day War, his rank clearly marked by the three slanting white stripes on his shirt sleeves. The uniform of a simple two-pocket shirt and trousers in olive drab was common across all branches of service, and only some paratroop units used camouflage clothing. Regulations stipulated that the shirts be worn open-necked, and it was permissible to have the sleeves rolled up even on parade. The trousers increasingly began to follow a narrower cut known as 'Taibas pants', a fashion choice that became common throughout the IDF of the period. The web gear worn by Uzi-armed troops used the same basic belt and suspenders, but with 5-cell SMG magazine pouches instead of the two 37 Ptn pouches of rifle-armed troops; it usually also supported a water bottle and a 2-cell grenade pouch. The Uzi is the 3.6kg wooden-stocked version (the stock could be removed quickly if the user desired – the variant with a metal folding butt had not yet been issued); it is chambered for 9x19mm Parabellum and fed by 25-round box magazines. First introduced to service in 1954, this simple, reliable and effective SMG was easy to handle in combat, being highly controllable even when fired fully-automatic.

Paratroopers return from a raid on Syrian military posts on the Kinneret (Sea of Galilee) in December 1955; the long olive-green cold-weather field jackets and trousers with cargo pockets are Israeli-made, and the tan web gear is British 37 Pattern surplus. The foreground soldier seems to carry a Mauser Kar 98K with a rifle-grenade adapter on the muzzle; his comrade to the left has a Belgian RL-83 *Blindicide* rocket launcher, and the man on the right the new Uzi sub-machine gun. While establishing consistent supplies of all arms was still a work in progress, there were particular shortfalls in anti-tank or anti-materiel weapons like bazookas, and rifle grenades were a cheap and relatively effective stopgap. (GPO)

The merger caused something of a culture shock to many in the old Bn 890, as Ariel Sharon set about remaking the battalion along the lines of Unit 101. Many officers transferred out to other commands, thus allowing Sharon to set his stamp on the battalion even more quickly. One officer who remained was Aharon Davidi, who quickly became invaluable as Sharon's second-in-command. Sharon and his band of irregulars brought with them fighting spirit matched by great skill and innovation in small-unit tactics, while Davidi supplied the knowledge of how to organize and run a full-strength regular army battalion. The fusion of the two cultures quickly led to the development of an unusually aggressive and militarily competent unit that was far ahead of other infantry units in the IDF (Luttwak & Horowitz 1975: 112). In 1956 the decision was taken to reorganize and expand the battalion into a brigade-strength force initially known as Unit 202 (later, 202 Paratroopers Bde) under Sharon's leadership. (Hereafter in this text we use the term 'Paratroopers Brigade', a literal translation from the Hebrew *Hativat HaTzanhanim*, but abbreviate it as 'Para Bde'.) The Nahal Bn 88, which had been training as parachute infantry under the command of Maj Mordechai 'Motta' Gur, joined the original Bn 890 and a newly established reserve unit, Bn 771, to complete the brigade's establishment. ('Nahal' is the acronym for *Noar Halutzi Lohem*, 'Fighting Pioneer Youth'. It was established in 1948 as a way for members of youth organizations to remain together during their period of military service. It became a distinct brigade of the IDF only in 1982.)

CHRONOLOGY

1948–49	Arab-Israeli War (also known as the War of Independence or the Palestine War)
1949	Paratroopers Battalion 890 founded
1953	Unit 101 founded
1954	Unit 101 absorbed into Bn 890
1956	Bn 890, Bn 771, & Bn 88 of the Nahal merge to form Unit 202, soon renamed 202 Paratroopers Brigade
1951–56	Reprisal actions against *fedayeen*

2 September 1948: Parachute 'commando' unit formed under the leadership of Yoel Palgi

1949: The first parachute unit is disbanded but quickly re-established as Paratroopers Battalion 890 under the command of Yehuda Harari

30 July 1953: Unit 101 formed under the command of Ariel Sharon

January 1954: Unit 101 merges with Battalion 890. Sharon takes over command of the newly combined force.

1955: The Nahal Parachute Infantry Unit. Renamed Battalion 88 in early 1956 after it joins Unit 202, it is again renamed as Battalion 50 after the 1956 Sinai campaign.

1955: Reserve Battalion 28. It is renamed Battalion 771 shortly after its transfer to Unit 202

November 1955: Battalion 890 is expanded by the addition of two more units, the Nahal Parachute Infantry Unit and Reserve Battalion 28. Initially called 'Unit 202' it quickly becomes 202 Paratroopers Brigade

1957: 202 Paratroopers Brigade is renamed 35 Paratroopers Brigade

1964: Battalion 771 is removed from 202 Paratroopers Brigade to form the cadre of 55 Paratroopers Brigade, which is formed the following year.

1964: Battalion 202, a newly raised regular parachute infantry unit, replaces Battalion 771.

1982: 35 Para Bde's recon company, *Sayeret Tzanhanim*, is reorganised as a battalion-sized force, *Gadsar Tzanhanim* (Battalion 5135)

1990: Battalion 50 leaves 35 Para Bde and returns to the Nahal Brigade.

1990: Battalion 101, a newly raised regular parachute infantry unit, replaces Battalion 50.

35 Paratroopers Brigade

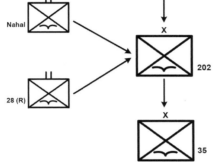

New recruits for the Paratroopers Brigade line up for issue of the famous red-brown jump boots at Tel Hashomer Induction Centre, Bakum, in 2013.

The current military service obligation is two years eight months for men (sometimes with a four-month extension) and two years for women. Unlike in other infantry brigades, service in the Para Bde is voluntary, requiring conscripts to apply for entry.

Israel's current active-duty strength stands at 160,000, with a further 630,000 serving in the reserves. There has been some discussion within the IDF about moving towards an all-volunteer army, but despite the benefits of higher levels of commitment and professionalism such an evolution would risk damaging the unusual depth and closeness of the relationship that the State of Israel still has with its soldiers. (GPO)

1956	Sinai Campaign/ Suez War (29 October–6 November): battle of the Mitla Pass
1957	202 Para Bde renumbered 35 Para Bde, although the old number remains in popular use for some time. 80 Para Bde (Reserve) founded, later renumbered 226 Para Bde
1965	55 Paratroopers Brigade (Reserve) founded
1967	Six-Day War against Egypt, Syria and Jordan (5–10 June)
1968–70	War of Attrition (Operations *Shock*, *Rooster 53* & *Rhodes*)
1973	Yom Kippur War (6–25 October – aka Ramadan War or October War)
1974	646 Paratroopers Brigade (Reserve) founded
1974	96 Division founded (later renumbered 98 Div)
1976	Entebbe Raid (Operation *Thunderbolt*, later renamed *Yonatan*)
1977	551 Paratroopers Brigade (Reserve) founded
1978	South Lebanon incursion (Operation *Litani*)
1982–85	First Lebanon War (Operation *Peace for Galilee*)
1985–2000	South Lebanon conflict continues
1987–91/93	First Intifada (West Bank & Gaza)
2000–04/05	Second Intifada ('Al Aqsa' Intifada, West Bank & Gaza)
2002	West Bank incursion (Operation *Defensive Shield*)
2004	Gaza incursions (Operations *Rainbow*, *Forward Shield* & *Days of Penitence*)
2006	Second Lebanon War (12 July–14 August)
2006	Gaza incursions (Operations *Summer Rain* & *Autumn Clouds*)
2008–09	Gaza War (Operation *Cast Lead*)
2012	Gaza Strip incursion (Operation *Pillar of Cloud*)
2014	Israel-Gaza conflict (Operation *Protective Edge*)
2015	89 '*Oz*' Commando Brigade formed

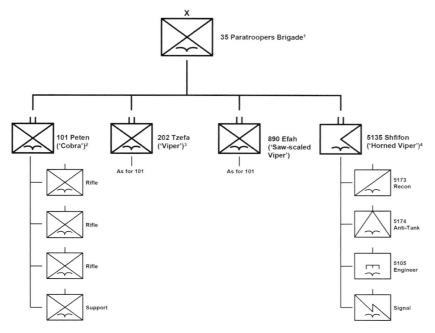

Organization of 35 Paratroopers Brigade, 2016

X

35 Paratroopers Brigade[1]

101 Peten ('Cobra')[2]

Rifle

Rifle

Rifle

Support

202 Tzefa ('Viper')[3]

As for 101

890 Efah ('Saw-scaled Viper')

As for 101

5135 Shfifon ('Horned Viper')[4]

5173 Recon

5174 Anti-Tank

5105 Engineer

Signal

1. Originally 202 Paratroopers Brigade, renamed 35 Paratroopers Brigade in 1957 after the Suez Crisis

2. Originally Battalion 88 (later Battalion 50) from the Nahal, it would remain part of 202's (later 35's) order of battle until 1990, whereupon a new unit – Battalion 101 – was raised to replace it.

3. Originally a reserve unit, Battalion 28 (later redesignated Battalion 771) was one of 202 Brigade's original units before it was detached to form the cadre of the new 55 Brigade. Battalion 202 was raised in 1964 as its replacement.

4. Formally established as *Gadsar Tzanhanim* (Battalion 5135) during the First Lebanon War

2005: recruits from the Paratroopers Brigade stretch out in exhaustion after a training march in rough country. Selection tests known as *Gibush Tzanhanim* are held twice a year in April and December. Following basic training the recruits must pass one final rite of passage: a 24-hour, 70km (43.5 mile) forced march, carrying weapons and full battle gear. Soldiers who complete this successfully are presented with their red berets, at a ceremony symbolizing their transformation from conscripts – even though volunteers for selection training – into paratroopers. (David Furst/AFP/Getty Images)

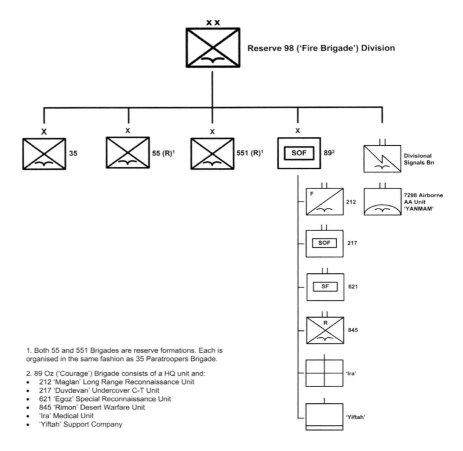

Reserve 98 ('Fire Brigade') Division

35

55 (R)[1]

551 (R)[1]

SOF   89[2]

Divisional Signals Bn

F   212

7298 Airborne AA Unit 'YANMAM'

SOF   217

SF   621

R   845

'Ira'

'Yiftah'

1. Both 55 and 551 Brigades are reserve formations. Each is organised in the same fashion as 35 Paratroopers Brigade.

2. 89 Oz ('Courage') Brigade consists of a HQ unit and:
- 212 'Maglan' Long Range Reconnaissance Unit
- 217 'Duvdevan' Undercover C-T Unit
- 621 'Egoz' Special Reconnaissance Unit
- 845 'Rimon' Desert Warfare Unit
- 'Ira' Medical Unit
- 'Yiftah' Support Company

A paratrooper awaits his turn to jump from a Hercules during a training exercise in 1997. While the modern incarnation of the Para Bde operates in more or less the same fashion as the IDF's other infantry formations, its focus on accepting only volunteers, coupled with the intensity of the training (which naturally includes passing the parachute qualification course), creates a strong sense of personal achievement, group identity and *esprit de corps*. Although the Mitla Pass drop in 1956 remains the IDF paratroopers' only unit-strength operational jump, parachute training continues. A major airborne practice drop took place in 2012, and another more extensive effort, involving the whole Para Bde and other special units complete with support vehicles, equipment, ammunition and supplies, is scheduled for 2018. (Avi Ohayon, GPO)

A female paratrooper prepares to go up for a training jump in March 2007. Despite their active role in the War of Independence, thereafter women were restricted from serving in combat roles until 2000. In that year the mixed-gender 33rd 'Caracal' Bn was raised; by 2009 it was 70 per cent female, and three more mostly female 'co-ed' battalions have since been created for border security duties. At the time of writing at least 2,700 women were serving in them (some physical standards have been lowered to ease basic training).

Though women currently make up 33 per cent of the IDF as a whole they only account for around 3 per cent of front-line forces, and this is an obvious factor in their relative scarcity in positions of seniority: most promotions to significant command require the officer to have experience in 'fighting' units. (Abir Sultan/ IDF via Getty Images)

ORGANIZATION

Recruitment and training

The methods of recruitment into today's Paratroopers Brigade have not changed greatly since the brigade's inception in the 1950s. Since 1949 Israel has operated a system of universal conscription for all men and women over the age of 18 (17 if the potential conscript requests it and obtains parental permission). Service was initially set at 24 months for men and 12 months for women, the current requirement being 32 months for men (subject to a potential 4-month extension) and 24 months for women. Around 40 per cent of the new recruits are medically assessed, with the best being filtered out for service in the infantry brigades, engineers and specialist field units. Exemptions to compulsory conscription exist for Arab citizens of Israel (something not available to the nation's other main ethnic groups – Jews, Druze and Circassians), and also for highly religious communities such as the ultra-orthodox Haredim, although exemptions on religious grounds have been increasingly sought by women in recent years. Today deferrals of service can be sought on academic grounds, for *yeshiva* students (often for so long that they are effectively exempted from service), or for young people who engage in a year of voluntary work in recognized youth organizations. Outright refusal to serve or 'draft-dodging' is still something of a rarity, though more common than it once was.

Unlike the other infantry brigades, service within the paratroopers is voluntary, with potential recruits put through a twice-yearly two-day selection process (*Gibush Tzanhanim*) to ensure that they can meet the physical and mental standards required. Training for recruits in 35 Para Bde is generally similar to that in the other infantry brigades (around 8 months of instruction in personal weapons proficiency, fieldcraft, intensive fitness and hand-to-hand combat), but with the inclusion of a compulsory two-week parachute course which is capped by a 70km (43.5 mile) all-night cross-country march in full gear. This *Masa Kumta* or 'beret march' ends in Jerusalem, after which the recruit has earned the right to wear the brigade's red beret. A further four months of advanced training is followed by active deployment.

Formations

The IDF's 35 Paratroopers Brigade is organized and equipped in a similar manner to the other regular infantry brigades (Golani, Givati, Nahal and Kfir). It consists of three paratroop battalions (all named after venomous snakes), each of three paratroop rifle companies and a support company, plus a reconnaissance battalion (*Gadsar Tzanhanim*) that has specialist reconnaissance, anti-tank, engineer and signals companies. Once the

C

INSIGNIA

(1) *Samal Rishon* of *Gadsar Tzanhanim*, 35 Paratroopers Brigade

This recon paratrooper is standing to attention in a formal parade during recent years, wearing his *Madei-Alef* ('Class A') uniform of a belted four-pocket tunic and trousers. His maroon-red beret is the traditional headgear of the paratroopers, inspired by the early association of the very first Israeli parachutists with British Airborne forces with whom they trained and operated during World War II. The bronze badge is a sword wrapped in an olive branch above a scroll, the insignia of the Infantry Corps, and is backed in scarlet-red. The tab that hangs from his left shoulder strap shows his parent formation, in this case the winged serpent of 35 Paratroopers Brigade. Shoulder tabs are only worn with Class A uniforms, and they vary in style according to unit and branch of service: those of corps and brigades end in a shield-point, regional commands and branches of service have rounded ends, while the Golani Brigade's tab is square-ended. The three rank chevrons adorned with a fig leaf on his sleeve mark him out as a *Samal Rishon* (staff sergeant), a rank usually attained only after at least 32 months' service. His status as a paratrooper is confirmed by the white metal jump wings worn over his left pocket; those shown here are backed with dark green cloth, denoting that he belongs to a reconnaissance unit. Rank-and-file jump wings are backed in dark blue, denoting the successful completion of the parachutist's course, including five successive jumps on the last day; a paratrooper who has taken part in a combat jump is allowed to change the backing to red. The first jump wings were made of embroidered cloth in a variety of designs, the transition to metal occurring around the same time that Battalion 890 merged with Unit 101 in early 1954. The pin just below the jump wings (a winged fleur-de-lis) is awarded for passing the selection course for the *Sayeret Tzanhanim* recon paratroopers, and the badge on his right pocket flap, also backed in green, shows his current affiliation to the *Gadsar Tzanhanim* (the regular Para Bde's reconnaissance battalion).

(2) *Rav Aluf* Benny Gantz, 2011

Lieutenant-General Gantz, who got his start in the Para Bde in 1977, was the IDF Chief of General Staff from 14 February 2011 until 16 February 2015. He wears the pale blue Class A dress shirt reserved for senior officers and staff, bearing a gilded sword-and-olive-branch command pin on the collar. He sports a paratrooper's beret tucked under his shoulder strap (always under the left shoulder strap, never the right). His rank of *Rav Aluf* is shown by the slip-on epaulette slides bearing a sword crossed with an olive branch surmounted by two fig leaves. The General Staff shoulder tab unites the symbols of the three armed services: a sword, wings and an anchor. Above his left breast pocket he wears a pair of senior paratrooper wings, as awarded to instructors or to those who have completed at least 50 jumps (including a minimum of 15 conducted at night and

30 during the day). His campaign ribbons, from his left to his right, denote service in the First (1982) and Second (2006) Lebanon Wars. On the pocket flap below them he wears the Combat Paratrooper Badge, awarded to those who fully complete all aspects of the paratrooper's 12-month training period. Above his right pocket he wears the pin for one of his old commands, Unit 5101, otherwise known as the *Shaldag* ('Kingfisher') unit; operating as a special forces group of the IAF, it was founded in 1974 with a responsibility for air-insertion into enemy territory to conduct reconnaissance, carry out commando raids, establish landing zones, and a variety of other specialist duties. On his right pocket flap he wears the operational service pin, granted to personnel with a minimum of six months' active operational service.

(3) Paratrooper *Samal Rishon* of 89 *Oz* Brigade, 2015

An operator with the rank of *Samal Rishon* from the *Rimon* Special Forces unit is seen at the time of his new brigade's formation ceremony in 2015. The shoulder tab (the double-headed arrow symbolizing their ability to be anywhere, the dagger their embrace of close combat) identifies the 89 *Oz* ('Courage') Brigade. Nicknamed the 'Commando' Brigade almost as soon as the idea was mooted, it became at a stroke one of the IDF's most potent assets, since it drew together four existing special operations units: *Maglan* (Unit 212), *Duvdevan* (Unit 217), *Egoz* (Unit 621) and *Rimon* (Unit 845). This soldier has gone through the paratrooper qualification process in order to win his jump wings, which are backed in blue rather than green (although he is a paratroop-trained special forces soldier, he does not serve within any of 35 Para Bde's special operations teams). Below them he wears a campaign ribbon from 2014's Operation *Protective Edge*. On the flap of his breast pocket he wears the silver Givati 'warrior' pin, which is awarded (in a similar fashion to the Combat Paratrooper badge) in recognition of a recruit's completion of all aspects of his training within that brigade, in addition to a 4-month tour of active duty.

(4) Captain Rafael Eitan, Battalion 890, November 1955

A figure harking back to the origins of the IDF paratroopers and of their insignia. Rafael 'Raful' Eitan was one of the small band of dynamic officers and men who were instrumental in founding the Israeli parachute force; he commanded a reserve paratroop company prior to Unit 101's merger with 890 in 1954. Shown here in the aftermath of Operation *Eged* (a successful cross-border night assault on an Egyptian outpost at Kunteila in the Sinai), he already wears the Infantry Corps badge on the maroon beret of the paratroops. In the earliest days there had been a few variations in cap badge for the new force, but by 1955 it seems the matter had been settled. His semi-cylindrical captain's bars (three on each epaulette) are in bronze metal. In the original photograph the insignia on the early version of the left shoulder tab is obscured, but it is most likely to be the winged viper (see Plate E1), which was designed in 1951 by Battalion 890's first commander, Yehuda Harari.

Aharon Davidi, a veteran of Israel's founding struggle and a key figure in the earliest days of the paratroopers, was Ariel Sharon's second-in-command after the merger of Unit 101 into Para Bn 890, and played a critical role in the battle for the Mitla Pass. He is pictured here on 8 June 1967, in the middle of the Six-Day War, when *Aluf Mishne* Davidi commanded a combined force of paratroopers and infantry responsible for the successful capture of Sharm-el-Sheik.

In January 1969, Col Davidi would be the first man appointed to the new post of Chief of Infantry and Paratroopers, a position that had evolved from his role as Chief Paratroop Officer (an appointment established in October 1965). The Chief Paratroop Officer was responsible for the professional guidance and organization of the paratroops, and for the parachute training school.

The IDF has always recognized the importance of first-class small-unit leadership, as exemplified by Davidi and the other aggressive officers of the original Para Bn 890, who cultivated an ethos of leading from the front and never ordering their men to undertake any task they would not be willing to fulfil themselves. This 'Follow me!' ethos led to high officer casualty figures (in senior as well as junior ranks), but the value of leading by personal example was never seriously questioned throughout the IDF's formative decades. (Micha Han, GPO)

paratroopers have completed their period of active service in the battalions of 35 Para Bde they are released into the reserves, being allocated to one of four brigades. These are the reserve 55 or reserve 551 Para Bdes, both of which are part of the reserve 98 'Fire Brigade' Division; the reserve 646 Para Bde, which is subordinate to the reserve 252 'Sinai' Division; and the reserve 226 Para Bde, which is subordinate to the reserve 319 Armoured Division.

Roles

Apart from the action at the Mitla Pass in 1956 there has been little call for the paratroopers to make much use of their eponymous skill in most of their engagements down the years, though there have been a number of occasions where combat jumps were planned (such as the prospective drop of 55 Para Bde on El Arish in the early stages of the Six-Day War) but called off at the last moment, usually due to rapidly developing circumstances – as has been the experience of many parachute units during and since World War II.

Airborne troops give a country great strategic reach, but initially had some significant downsides – most notably, a lack of integral heavy weapons, very low mobility once dropped, and the likely need to supply and support them by air until they can link up with ground forces. The development of helicopter-borne operations, as pioneered by the French in Algeria and the Americans in Vietnam, offered partial solutions to all of those problems, and the Israelis did make limited use of this new tactic in the quickly developing situations of the 1967 and 1973 wars. The arrival of the helicopter provided an efficient platform to insert (and evacuate) troops, making many smaller-scale operations more easily staged with rotors than with silk and fixed-wing transports. The capability to launch vertical envelopments remained, whether using helicopters or fixed-wing aircraft, but the circumstances for a brigade-scale deployment have never yet materialized.

Even with their feet firmly on the ground the Paratroopers Brigade was still a significant force when deployed as elite mechanized infantry, rolling across the Sinai or up to the Golan Heights in M3 half-tracks in 1967 – a role that they would continue to fulfil in later conflicts including the 1982 invasion of Lebanon and beyond, albeit with more modern vehicles. Despite

the utility of such a role on even the most modern of battlefields, the success of armour in the Six-Day War would lead to a general diminishment of the perceived value of infantry (paratroopers included) within the IDF. This mistake was shown up disastrously during the Yom Kippur War six short years later. The rebalancing of the armoured brigades would take some time, with doctrine lagging behind necessity well into the 1980s. The nature of the wars that the paratroopers found themselves fighting began to change during this period, moving away from the high-intensity conventional wars of the 1960s and 1970s and towards drawn-out asymmetric conflicts with militias or popular insurgencies in occupied territories. Such new problems would demand new solutions.

A paratrooper heavy machine-gun crew fire their .50cal M2 Browning during a summer training exercise in 1965; the gunner wears a mixed outfit of olive-green shirt with French M47 'lizard-pattern' camouflage trousers. In the IDF the M2 has been as popular and reliable a weapon as in every other army that has used it. Tripod-mounted guns were usually set up as part of a prepared defensive position, being too cumbersome to carry any distance in an assault. The heavy-barrelled M2HB version that was mounted on the ubiquitous M3 half-track was used to provide supporting fire for dismounted paratroopers. (Moshe Milner, GPO)

OPERATIONS, 1956–1978

The Mitla Pass, 1956
Gamal Abdel Nasser, newly installed as President of Egypt, had unleashed a tide of Egyptian and Arab nationalism at a stroke with his seizure of the Suez Canal. Snubbing British and French interests in equal measure, Nasser also provoked Israel when he blockaded the Gulf of Aqaba and closed the Straits of Tiran to Israeli shipping. A covert Anglo-French scheme was soon developed to wrest control of the Canal back from the Egyptians, and Israel's part in the coordinated plan would be to encircle and capture the whole of the Sinai Peninsula.

The Six-Day War saw 'Raful' Eitan's 35 Para Bde (still often called '202' by many, including Eitan) deployed in half-tracks as part of Gen Tal's 84 Armd Div on the Gaza and Sinai front. The M3 half-track was in widespread Israeli use throughout the 1950s and 1960s, and still played an important battlefield role during the Yom Kippur War, though it was then slowly being replaced with the unpopular M113 APC. M3s (all variants were designated 'M3' in IDF service, whatever their original identity) mounted a range of machine guns, primarily the Browning .30cal M1919A4 or the .50cal M2HB seen here, as well as 81mm and 120mm mortars when in the support role. This paratroop unit was photographed while concentrating at Nebi Mussa for spring manoeuvres in 1970; the half-tracks still bear the ground-air recognition markings used in 1967. (Moshe Milner, GPO)

One of the key stages involved air-dropping Battalion 890 under LtCol Rafael Eitan on to the Mitla Pass close to the eastern bank of the Canal, to cut Egyptian supply lines for their forces positioned in the eastern quarter of the Sinai Peninsula. Once on the ground the paratroopers would be over 130 miles inside Egyptian territory, with the mission of holding the Pass until a relief column of trucks and half-tracks carrying the rest of 202 Para Bde under Ariel Sharon could reach them. The strategy was bold and relied heavily on the calibre of the troops involved for its success (more so than was originally anticipated, due to communications and logistical problems that arose from the speed and scope of the operation). In the event, the parachute operation was integral to the IDF's seizure of the whole of the Sinai in little over 100 hours, through an audacious and entirely unexpected series of manoeuvres.

The drop from 16 Douglas C-47 Dakotas was made at 1700hrs on 29 October 1956, and Eitan's men landed outside their drop zone, 5 miles distant from their objective of the Heitan Defile. They moved into position, and were supplied that same evening by an airdrop of some light weapons and jeeps to help bolster their defence against Egyptian probes that had already begun, launched from positions within the Pass. Early relief of Eitan's highly exposed paratroopers was obviously critically important, and Sharon had promised to cross the Sinai within a day. Around 28 hours after the first paratrooper's boots had hit the rough sands of the Sinai, Sharon's column arrived, having fought its way through several minor skirmishes during its headlong 125-mile westwards drive from Kuntilla.

With their objective secured, 202 Para Bde should have taken up a defensive position, but Sharon was keen to push through into the Pass

Aluf Haim Bar-Lev, Deputy Chief of Staff, *Aluf* Ariel Sharon, commanding 38 Armd Bde, and *Aluf* Yishayahu Gavish, Southern Command, arriving by Sikorsky helicopter in the Negev Desert, 1 June 1967. The dress of general officers has always been as varied and often as modest as that worn by the rank-and-file, with little other than shoulder-strap slides to distinguish them. In more modern times senior staff have adopted a pale blue dress shirt, but for use with the Class A uniform only. (David Rubinger, GPO)

proper. Refused permission to do so by Gen Moshe Dayan (Chief of the General Staff), Sharon instead secured his agreement that he send out a reconnaissance patrol on 31 October. In fact, the force he ordered into the Pass was much more significant, resembling a mechanized battalion combat team supported by a small escort of AMX-13 tanks.

The 'patrol' entered the Pass, its lead elements reaching the far end before the Egyptians (who had five companies well established in a series of positions along the sides of the Pass, supported by machine guns and light weapons) sprung their ambush. The majority of the Israelis found

A group of paratroopers pose for a captain's camera in the act of hanging the Israeli flag to a fence on the Temple Mount in Jerusalem, 7 June 1967. They wear a motley collection of uniforms, but all appear to be armed with wooden-stocked Uzis; the version with the collapsible metal butt did not appear until shortly after the Six-Day War. (GPO)

themselves pinned down, their vehicles hit repeatedly, many burning, and with numbers of wounded and dead paratroopers increasing with each passing hour. Mostly equipped only with short-range Uzi sub-machine guns, the paratroopers lacked the weaponry to fight their way up to the Egyptian positions on the ridges. Their position was bolstered only when Sharon sent through some reinforcements that helped to evacuate the wounded. The fight continued into the night, with the paratroopers attacking both ends of the Pass simultaneously: the western end by the lead elements of the initial column, who had made it through before being engaged, and the eastern end by a further two companies of reinforcements from the brigade. The battle came down to a series of close engagements, some involving hand-to-hand combat, until the resolve of the Egyptian defenders finally broke and they withdrew from the Pass. The paratroopers did not hold their newly won ground, instead withdrawing back to their original positions, at a cost of 38 dead and 120 wounded.

Though they had beaten a determined force in well-sited positions with the advantage of terrain and surprise, the IDF remembered the battle as much for the fact that it was unnecessary as for the overall tactical success of the parachute operation of which it was a part. Sharon faced no consequences for his actions; Dayan preferred headstrong stallions to recalcitrant mules, and the overall success of the Sinai campaign obscured some potentially serious problems within the IDF. Communications were unreliable, and exacerbated a habit for individual brigades to fight their own battles rather than to play their part in the larger operational plan under a coherent chain of command. Armoured formations were underemployed, and there was no consistent method of merging infantry and tanks into effective combined-arms battlegroups. The paratroopers had proved the value of their ethos and training, and their success led to the establishment of two more reserve paratroop brigades prior to the Six-Day War 11 years later. However, their tactics were still focused on small-scale actions relying on movement instead of firepower. This was effective in many situations, but emblematic of the IDF's *ad hoc* approach to the development of a consistent doctrine that could make much more of the skill and professionalism that such units displayed.

Six days in 1967: Um Katef

The lightning pre-emptive war launched by Israel on 5 June 1967 against Egypt, Jordan and Syria, at the climax to a strategic game of brinksmanship that had got out of hand, would see the paratroopers committed on all three fronts, though only in Jerusalem would they operate as an independent infantry force.

The regular 35 Paratroopers Brigade, now under the command of 'Raful' Eitan, was a part of Gen Israel Tal's 84 Armoured Division; it was freshly issued with M3 half-tracks stripped by Tal from his division's integral mechanized infantry because the paratroopers, though not specifically trained in mechanized tactics, were considered better fighters. Eitan's brigade was instrumental in the outflanking and capture of Rafah near Gaza on the coast road, though a more dramatic role awaited the reservists of Col Danni Matt's 80 Paratroopers Brigade.

Ariel Sharon, now commanding 38 Armd Bde, was operating to the south of Tal's force and was tasked with breaking into the central Sinai. This required the capture of the road junction at Abu-Ageila, sited less than

20 miles from the Israeli border. The Egyptians were well aware of the site's importance (it had been fought over in 1948 and again in 1956), and had concentrated their deployment of an infantry division supplemented with strong contingents of armour and artillery around Abu-Ageila itself and the plateau of Um Katef that lay a little to the east of the junction. Sharon, rather than relying upon the traditionally mercurial Israeli methods of manoeuvre and adaptation in the face of the enemy, opted for a rigidly planned operation. This was partly because the Egyptian dispositions had been unusually well reconnoitred, and partly because variants of this very attack had been fought time and again at the IDF staff college, aware as they were of their failure to break though in this same area in the 1956 war. Sharon thus had all the intelligence and contingency plans he could wish for, allowing him to execute an unusually bold, highly choreographed assault involving all the elements of his division.

As night fell on 5 June 1967, Sharon's armour and infantry launched a series of well-coordinated thrusts at specifically chosen sections of the Egyptian position, attacking from the northern dunes which the Egyptians had thought impassable. A key element in the whole assault was the neutralization of the Egyptian artillery, of which six battalions stood at Um Katef behind the main position, ready to unleash havoc on any attacker – and this was the objective for the paratroopers.

A paratroop signaller seen during the March 1970 manoeuvres; he wears the old British Airborne helmet with web strapping, and a so-called 'Bar-Lev' padded winter jacket with fleece lining and collar and knit cuffs, as popularized by that general. The standard radio used by infantry at company level and below was the American PRC-25; weighing 25lbs including battery and accessories, it had a range of 3 to 5 miles, and a 60-hour battery life when using the portable BA-4386 power supply. Though quickly obsolescent in the US Army, the 'Prick-25' and its very similar successor the PRC-77 would not be superseded in IDF service until the late 1990s, when new digital sets began to be adopted. The modern force uses a variety of NATO-compliant models such as the PRC-148 and PRC-152, among others. (Moshe Milner, GPO)

Colonel Danni Matt and a battalion of paratroopers flew across the desert in a squadron of Sikorsky S-58 helicopters, landing a little over a mile from their target. Making their way through the darkness towards the Egyptian guns (they were specially trained in night operations), the paratroopers were surprised to find no minefields or wire obstacles to hamper their progress; they soon fell upon their objective, attacking from gun position to gun position. The surprise and ferocity of this night assault caused chaos among the Egyptians; guns were abandoned, positions quickly overrun, bunkers destroyed, and an ammunition supply column that wandered into the middle of the battle was cut to pieces. The paratroopers effectively neutralized the Egyptian artillery just prior to the Israeli division's main assault, destabilizing the whole defensive line.

Jerusalem

The success of the Southern Command in driving into the Sinai had an important knock-on effect for one unit, 55 Para Bde under the command of Col Mordechai 'Motta' Gur. They were initially tasked with jumping onto the airfield at El Arish on the northern coast of the Sinai, but the breakneck progress of Israel Tal's division had already reached that objective on the first day, making such an operation unnecessary. As a result, the brigade found itself seconded to the Central Command, which would allow an assault on the Jordanian forces that held the environs of eastern Jerusalem. Arriving

with Central Command on the evening of 5 June, the paratroopers had to raid the stocks of local forces to replace much of the equipment that they had had to leave behind in their rush to redeploy, much of it still packed on pallets ready for the cancelled drop on El Arish.

A plan of attack was pulled together in a matter of hours, with a more or less immediate night assault being seen as having the best chance of success. Gur's brigade was to take the Arab sector north of the Old City, including the Police Academy, Ammunition Hill (so-called from its use as an ammunition storage depot during the Mandate), and an area just south of that hill known as the American Colony. Defended by well-trained and competent Jordanian troops, Ammunition Hill in particular was strongly protected by a network of trenches supported by several bunkers, many covered positions and a recoilless rifle, the whole emplacement being surrounded by wire entanglements.

At 2200hrs on 5 June a sharp artillery bombardment heralded an attack by all three of 55 Bde's units (Bns 66, 71 and 28); the outlying wire was breached easily enough with Bangalore torpedoes, but the densely interconnected nature of the Jordanian defences meant that progress was slow and arduous, the attackers having to take one bunker or position at a time. Such fighting, whose outcomes were decided at close range with small arms and grenades, required courage, tenacity and skill. The Police Academy was eventually taken, and focus shifted to Ammunition Hill, which the companies of Bn 66 attacked from three sides with the support of a platoon of Sherman tanks. Intense fighting lasted until daybreak on 6 June, whereupon the growing light allowed the Israeli tanks to target remaining Jordanian bunkers with point-blank fire, destroying them one after another. Just to the south, Bns 71 and 28 had captured the American Colony, and the whole area was pacified by 1000hrs.

This allowed the paratroopers, in concert with 10 'Harel' Mechanized Bde, to spend the remainder of the day securing the eastern approaches

An IAF Super Frelon helicopter waiting to lift troops and equipment after the successful completion of the raid on Shadwan Island, January 1970. The War of Attrition that followed the Six-Day War, mostly fought over the ceasefire line in the Sinai, would last until 1970. Although it was a 'low-intensity' conflict it would cost more than 2,000 Israeli casualties, including 694 killed in action. (Moshe Milner, GPO)

A Galil ARM, which would serve the IDF from its introduction in late 1973 through to the 2000s. Probably the weapon's best-known feature was the deliberate design of the bipod retention lug to double as a bottle opener. Israeli soldiers had been in the habit of using the lips of their rifle magazines to prize off bottle caps, thus causing an entirely predictable increase in malfunctions due to feeding problems. (Yaacov Saar, GPO)

D

LEBANON & GAZA, 1978–1992
(1) Paratrooper, Battalion 890; Operation *Litani*, Lebanon, 1978

This trooper, who has just alighted from a helicopter, wears an M76 pattern helmet with netting and black rubber band, and the 'Ephod' load-bearing system, which first saw action two years previously at Entebbe in Operation *Thunderbolt*. The Ephod (named after an ancient garment worn by high priests) was much more comfortable than the old webbing gear that it replaced. It consisted of a pair of broad vertical suspender straps with a yoke piece, supporting sets of three or four pouches of differing size on fabric backing pieces, plus a single large rear central pouch; the three components were linked horizontally by double and triple narrow straps instead of being attached to a conventional belt. It allowed the trooper to carry a dozen 5.56mm magazines, as well as grenades, medical supplies and other sundries, and offered a degree of 'modularity' – it could be rigged according to personal preference. His personal weapon is the Galil ARM (Assault Rifle & Machine-Gun), introduced in late 1972 but initially in such small numbers that its use was negligible in the Yom Kippur War. Designed as both an assault rifle and squad support weapon, the Galil ARM fell between two stools; the requirement to function as a light support weapon meant that it was heavier than comparable 5.56x45mm rifles (4.35kg, against the 3.4kg of a loaded M16A2). In the support role its original 50-round magazine was too large to operate comfortably when prone, being replaced by the standard 35-round magazine in most situations. Later variations would enjoy more success, but the Galil was never a really popular weapon, and its design made it difficult to upgrade with new optics or additional mountings, especially when compared with the more modular platform offered by American rifles. Many of the IDF's specialist reconnaissance units opted to use the M16/CAR-15 instead, and some even preferred captured AKMs/AK-74s over the Galil. This trooper also carries a British 2in (52mm) Mk VIII mortar, predominantly used for firing smoke or illumination rounds.

(2) Marksman, Battalion 890; South Lebanon, 1981

This member of a reconnaissance platoon on patrol in the rough mountainous terrain of Lebanon has just spotted a target and has raised his rifle for a snap shot. He wears a battered 'Kova Raful' fatigue hat, a 'woolly pully' jumper (a popular item in the chilly mountains), and OG-107 fatigue trousers, a legacy of US imports in the 1970s that were uncommon but (unaccountably) sought-after. His equipment

and ammunition is stored in his Ephod system, which accommodates the 20-round magazines for his M21 rifle. Israel's sniping capability diverged into two separate tracks during the 1970s and early 1980s. When the time came to replace the venerable British Enfield No. 4 Mk 1 (T) the IDF opted to adapt some of the M14s provided in relatively large numbers in US airlifts – Operation *Nickel Grass* – during the Yom Kippur War. This programme would follow that of the US Army, modifying M14s into M21 semi-automatic sniper rifles (though in fact this was a designated marksman's weapon rather than a true sniper rifle, leading the IDF to make additional *ad hoc* procurements of dedicated 'Sniper Weapon Systems'). The selected M14s were adapted to fire semi-automatically only, and fitted with a cheek-piece and rubber butt-pad, an adjustable bipod for the forestock, and a Japanese-made El-Op 6x40 Nimrod scope of black anodized aluminium. The M21 was good out to 690m (750yds) when using match-grade M118 NATO 7.62mm ammunition, though the rigours of field use made such a long reach an occasional rather than a regular occurrence. The M21 would finally be superseded in 1997 by the M24 SWS based on the Remington Model 700.

(3a) Paratrooper with B-300 rocket launcher; Gaza border, 1992

This patrolling trooper, wearing an M76/85 helmet, has 'taken a knee' to load a round into his rocket launcher; his personal weapon is a G'lilon SAR (the shortened folding-stock variant of the Galil) slung across his back. Entering service in 1980, the B-300 mainly found favour with IDF paratroop and special forces units thanks to its versatile rounds and compact profile; it is light (3.65kg, or 8kg loaded) and only 0.76m long when unloaded. This reusable rocket launcher can fire either 82mm HEAT (High-Explosive Anti-Tank) warheads against armour, or HEFT (High-Explosive Follow-Through) warheads against structures and personnel, out to a maximum range of 300m (using the optical sight). The HEAT round is conventional, though its performance drops off against newer vehicles with better or reactive armour. The HEFT rocket operates by a two-stage process: it first punches through walls or soft armour, and then detonates a secondary anti-personnel charge.

(3b) Carrying the launcher slung, and spare rounds on a packboard. The rockets are kept in sealed, airtight fibreglass containers that act as the rear part of the launching system once they are loaded into the B-300, being discarded after firing.

A helicopter-inserted detachment of paratroopers trek across the Jordanian border at Wadi Firdan in pursuit of a group of El Fatah fighters, 1968. The periods between the major wars of 1956, 1967, 1973 and 1982 were rarely peaceful, with a constant series of tit-for-tat incursions and counter-attacks back and forth across Israel's borders. As well as confrontations with Egypt, Israel also faced incursions from Jordan, Syria and South Lebanon throughout the 1970s, and responded with retaliatory attacks which often took troops well beyond the borders. (Eli Landau, GPO)

to Jerusalem, cutting the city off from Jordanian support. The following morning, 7 June, at 0930hrs Motta Gur led his paratroopers, piled into half-tracks along with their supporting armour, through the Lion's Gate and into the Old City, encountering only desultory resistance before reaching the Western Wall half an hour later; they thus secured one of the most totemic victories in Israeli history.

Aside from the notable achievement of the paratroopers in the capture of Jerusalem, much of the credit for the successes of the war went to the armoured brigades. Their performance had been impressive, but there were mitigating factors (not the least of which was the tactics and competence of their opponents) that gave a false picture of their true utility. Seeing future victories as dependent on an ever-stronger armoured corps, the IDF would neglect the role of infantry, including paratroopers, over the coming years. For the paratroopers the near future would come to be defined more by counter-insurgency and special operations than by any focus on what their role ought to be in a new conventional war, and the eventual cost of this neglect would be high.

Attrition and insurgency, 1968–1970

The seemingly glorious conclusion of the Six-Day War brought no secure peace. The Egyptians under Nasser refused to accept the disastrous loss of the Sinai, embarking on what would become known as the War of Attrition; this low-intensity conflict would eventually spread to the Jordanian and Syrian borders, and would last until 1970.

At the same time Palestinian resistance to Israel developed apace in neighbouring countries, focused most notably in Jordan in the late

1960s. In an echo of earlier times the Palestinians (in addition to laying mines and launching occasional rocket attacks on Israeli settlements) launched cross-border incursions by sabotage units into the occupied West Bank. This was effectively countered by a two-pronged IDF strategy. Firstly, careful observation of movement along the border, supported by the efforts of Bedouin trackers, allowed the Israelis to develop a good picture of when and where insurgent groups were crossing. Secondly, specially selected units of paratroopers were stationed in the Jordan Valley, and as soon as an infiltration was detected and tracked they would interdict the group by helicopter-borne insertions.

The IDF could also be proactive, as demonstrated by Operation *Tofet* on 21 March 1968. This saw a strong force of paratroopers (Bns 202 and 50, as well as the recon unit *Sayeret Tzanhanim*), supported by armour, striking across the Jordanian border to one of the major Palestinian training bases at Karameh. They effectively destroyed it, though at a more substantial cost than they would have liked. Eventually the unacceptably high rate of failure that the Palestinians endured in such actions, coupled with a growing impatience on the part of the Jordanian government at the larger costs that such behaviour on their territory incurred, led the Jordanians to force the Palestinians out in 1970. Their organizations eventually decamped to southern Lebanon, where their campaigns (including straightforward terrorist actions) would continue apace.

On 17 October 1973, during the Yom Kippur War, the former Chief of Staff Haim Bar-Lev confers with a bandaged Ariel Sharon, then commanding 143 Armoured Division. A fundamental figure in paratroop operations in all Israel's wars from 1956 to 1973, Sharon was undoubtedly a precociously talented commander, but also a headstrong and disobedient one who could drive his superiors to distraction, and his adventures were not always excused by success. As Minister of Defence he would be one of the key players in the decision to invade Lebanon in 1982, an operation which ultimately proved to be badly planned and ill thought-through. (Yossi Greenberg, GPO)

The Six-Day War had exposed the need to improve infantry training across the board, and on 1 January 1969 Col Aharon Davidi's role of Chief Paratroop Officer was expanded into Chief of Infantry and Paratroopers. This decision sent a clear signal that the paratroopers were still firmly at the forefront of the IDF's infantry establishment.

This period also saw a greater development of the paratroopers' role in the execution of special operations of a greater range and complexity than had characterized their counter-insurgency activities in the 1950s and early 1960s. Operation *Shock*, conducted on 31 October 1968 by a helicopter-borne detachment of *Sayeret Tzanhanim*, was a deep-penetration attack on Egyptian electrical infrastructure in response to cross-border artillery barrages that had killed numbers of Israeli soldiers. Resulting in irreparable damage to the Qena bridge, as well as destroying a large number of transformers and damaging the Nag-Hammadi dam, the operation gave a taste of what was to come. Operation *Rooster 53*, launched in December 1969, involved paratroopers from Bn 50 as well as a detachment from *Sayeret Tzanhanim* tasked with the capture of a newly installed Egyptian

P-12 radar system at Ras Gharib. This mission was executed flawlessly, with the dismantled radar flown back to Israel for inspection. Less than a month later, on 22 January 1970 a combined force of paratroopers from Bn 202 and *Sayeret Tzanhanim* in concert with a detachment of naval commandos from *Shayetet 13* launched Operation *Rhodes*, an audacious temporary seizure of Shadwan Island in the Gulf of Suez, resulting in the capture of 62 prisoners and the destruction of all the island's buildings apart from its lighthouse.

Yom Kippur, 1973

The wars of the previous decades had seen the IDF excel in battalion- and later brigade-level actions, but the scope of the military problems that confronted them in 1973 would require a deeper level of operational ability than they had previously developed. The attacks by Syria into the Golan Heights and by Egypt across the Suez Canal on 6 October 1973 caught Israel by complete surprise, and for the first few days the situation was more serious than at any other time in the state's history, before or since. In the event, though at heavy cost, both fronts were able to withstand the worst of the initial onslaughts, giving reserve units time to mobilize and

Yonatan 'Yoni' Netanyahu, who was the only IDF fatality when he led the breaching force of paratroopers and *Sayeret Matkal* in their successful rescue of hostages from Entebbe airport in Uganda in July 1976, had already proved himself to be one of Israel's ablest soldiers. Originally joining the paratroopers in 1964, he rose to command a company, and in the Six-Day War acquitted himself well both at the battle of Um Katef and on the Golan Heights. By the 1973 Yom Kippur War he was leading the *Sayeret Matkal*, Israel's premier reconnaissance and counter-terrorist unit, which played a crucial part in the recapture of Mount Hermon from Syrian commandos in the dying days of that conflict. He spent a short time after the war in command of the 'Barak' Armd Bde on the Golan – a striking example of the IDF's characteristic flexibility in command appointments – before returning to special operations. (GPO)

deploy and thus to some extent stabilizing what was still a military crisis.

In Suez the initial Egyptian successes were eventually checked, and their army quickly assumed a defensive posture to secure the gains they had made after their initial crossing of the Canal. Troops from 35 Para Bde, barely out of training, were sent to the southern Sinai to hunt down Egyptian helicopter-borne commandos which had made a nuisance of themselves, while Danni Matt's 247 Para Bde was attached to Ariel Sharon's 143 Armoured Division. There it would play a crucial role in Operation *Gazelle*, the Israeli attempt to secure a counter-crossing to the west bank of the Canal. There was a gap between the Egyptian Second and Third Armies that Sharon was eager to exploit, by driving between the two forces and crossing to the Egyptian side of the Canal to dislocate their whole defensive line. Everything about the operation was fraught with difficulty and required bold and effective leadership; the key role was given to Danni Matt, who would lead 750 paratroopers from his brigade across the Canal in rubber dinghies, securing both banks to allow for the laying of a Bailey bridge.

Under the codename Operation *Valiant*, on the night of 15/16 October Matt's paratroopers, often under heavy fire, reached the Canal and crossed successfully at Deversoir at about 0130hrs. By dawn the whole brigade had made it across to establish a bridgehead; armoured support soon started rolling across the bridge, making its presence felt among the shocked Egyptian defenders. That signal success, valuable as it was, remained at the mercy of the situation on the eastern bank of the Canal, particularly in an area a few miles north of the crossing point known as the Chinese Farm (an abandoned agricultural station that had been manned by Japanese agronomists, its name due to the markings they left on the site's buildings being misinterpreted as Chinese). Elements from the much-mauled Egyptian 21 Armoured Div, supported by 16 Infantry Div, began to move south intent on destroying the

Israeli position on the eastern bank. Colonel Uzi Yairi's 35 Para Bde was sent on 15 October to clear the area of the Chinese Farm that lay between the Egyptians and the Israeli bridgehead.

The initial reconnaissance conducted by a paratrooper company ran into surprisingly stiff resistance, requiring support from two more companies, and eventually the rest of the brigade. The two sides dug in, often as little as 100yds apart, and exchanged intense and unrelenting fire. The Egyptian attacks were conducted with small arms but also rocket-propelled grenades and AT-3 Saggers (9M14 Malyutka), which were available to the Egyptian Army in such quantities that some of them were fired at individual Israeli soldiers. By nightfall the battle had see-sawed for 14 hours and the Egyptians were spent, though it would take several more days and more Israeli reinforcements before they were finally driven from their defensive positions at the Farm, at the cost to 35 Bde of over 50 dead and 100 wounded.

On the Syrian front, the battle for the Golan was a ferocious armoured duel in which infantry played a relatively minor part, at least until the Israelis managed to push the Syrians back over the border and began their pursuit. Two battalions of 317 Para Bde in concert with Yoni Netanyahu's *Sayeret Matkal* played an important part in the eventual Israeli recapture of Mount Hermon from the Syrian 82 and 183 Commando Bns, which had seized the IDF's observation post during the first hours of the war. The paratroopers' skill in small-unit tactics was augmented by the daring nature of the assault, with the battalions (625 paratroopers in total) inserted by helicopter behind the main Syrian positions on the mountain, bottling them up and cutting

Israeli Defence Minister Shimon Peres (left) and *Tat aluf* Dan Shomron (second left) with Israeli paratroops after the completion of Operation *Thunderbolt*, July 1976. The Entebbe Airport raid resulted in the rescue of 102 hostages held by members of the Popular Front for the Liberation of Palestine, at the cost of one Israeli soldier and three hostages killed. All the terrorists died, as well as an undetermined number of Ugandan soldiers who were guarding the airport for them. (Keystone/Hulton Archive/ Getty Images)

off any chance of reinforcement. An infantry force of the Golani Bde then assaulted up the south-eastern face of the mountain, eventually fighting their way to the top and destroying the Syrian defenders in a bloody and merciless engagement.

Despite Israel's success in fending off massive attacks on two fronts in little more than a fortnight, the 1973 War was a deep shock to the nation and the army. The conflict demonstrated a relative inflexibility of thought at the higher echelons of the IDF, as well as a certain lack of consistency in working together towards a common cause – something exacerbated by several of the outsize personalities involved, such as Ariel Sharon. Intelligence failures had been cruelly exposed, as had the folly of developing armoured forces denuded of integral infantry, and even denied the proper training to work with separate infantry units. The high toll taken by Syrian and Egyptian

E

FORMATION INSIGNIA
(1) 35 Paratroopers Brigade (Regular)
The 'Winged Serpents' are the only regular paratroop brigade in the IDF, and are administratively subordinate to the 'Fire Brigade' – 98 Paratroopers Division (Reserve). The 'winged serpent' motif comes from a biblical verse that Prime Minister David Ben-Gurion recited to the first paratroopers upon their establishment, suggesting that the intelligence and cunning of the snake should be an inspiration to them in their service. The training regime of 35 Para Bde is heavy: seven and a half months of training and a two-week parachuting qualification course, all capped by a 70km forced march to win the right to wear the beret, after which the recruit undergoes a further period of advanced training in either the Northern or Southern theatres. Despite some early teething troubles among the embryo parachute unit, 35 Para Bde traces its roots back to 1948, and all the major features of the IDF paratroop units (including the evolution of distinctive items of uniform, as well as professionalism, aggression and *esprit de corps*) were well in place by the mid-1950s. The impact made on the IDF as a whole by the officers and men who have passed through the battalions of this single brigade is out of all proportion to their modest numbers. When members of the brigade complete their military service and return home they are reassigned to one of the reserve para brigades, ideally the one nearest to where they happen to live.

(2) 55 Paratroopers Brigade (Reserve)
Nicknamed the 'Tip of the Spear', 55 Para Bde officially came into being in 1965, and is administratively subordinate to the 98 Paratroopers Division (Reserve). Soldiers of the brigade were heavily involved in the fighting for Jerusalem in 1967 and were instrumental in the capture of the Old City after the battle of Ammunition Hill. Renumbered 247 Para Bde in 1969, the formation moved to Southern Command throughout the War of Attrition, defending the banks of the Suez Canal. The counter-attacks against the Egyptian onslaught in 1973 saw units of the brigade take part in Ariel Sharon's Operation *Gazelle*, crossing the Canal and securing bridgeheads. In the wake of the Yom Kippur War the formation was again renumbered (to 623 Para Bde) and fought in some fashion throughout all the various conflicts of the succeeding decades. They eventually returned to their original designation '55' in 2006, after the end of the Second Lebanon War.

(3) 551 Paratroopers Brigade (Reserve)
The 551 ('Arrows of Fire') Brigade, also a subordinate formation of 98 Para Div (Reserve), grew out of Battalion 697 – a unit founded by Rafael Eitan in 1968 – and was always based on reservists from 35 Para Bde and other special operations units. It fought in the Yom Kippur War on the Sinai front, where it gained experience in the use of BGM-71 TOW missiles; this encouraged the brigade's development as a force primarily concerned with anti-tank warfare. It fought in both Lebanon Wars (though only as infantry in the Second), but since then it has continued to develop its distinctive focus on AT capabilities.

(4) 646 Paratroopers Brigade (Reserve)
The 646 (nicknamed the 'Sky Foxes') was formed in 1974 in the wake of the Yom Kippur War, and went on to serve in the First Lebanon War (1982), after which it continued to operate for long periods in the South Lebanon security zone. It was engaged against the First Intifada in Gaza, and was also involved in Operation *Cast Lead* in 2008–09. Since 2000 it has been subordinate to 252 'Sinai' Division (Reserve).

(5) 226 Paratroopers Brigade (Reserve)
Known as the 'Eagles' or the Northern Paratroop Brigade, 226 is subordinate to 319 Armoured Division (Reserve) and operates under the Northern Command. The oldest and first in precedence among the reserve paratroop brigades, 226 was formed in 1957 (initially as 80 Para Bde, and subsequently undergoing a series of redesignations as 317, then 939, until it finally settled on 226). It served in the Six-Day War under Col Danni Matt, making a significant contribution to Ariel Sharon's attack through the Sinai before being rapidly transferred to help secure the Golan. It was heavily engaged on both Northern and Southern fronts during the Yom Kippur War, particularly at the crossing of the Suez Canal. It would go on to serve in both Lebanon Wars as well as against the Second Intifada.

(6) 98 Paratroopers Division (Reserve)
Also known as the 'Fire Brigade', 98 Para Div was established in 1974 (initially numbered 96 Div); it is a mix of regular and reserve paratroop infantry formations, subordinated to the Central Command. The division is administratively the parent of the regular 35 Paratroopers Brigade and the newly founded (in 2015) 89 Oz or 'Commando' Brigade, as well as the 55 and 551 Para Bdes (Reserve), the 7298 'YANMAM' Airborne Anti-Aircraft Unit, and a signals battalion.

1

2

3

5

6

anti-tank teams armed with AT-3 Sagger missiles had highlighted the need for infantry to work in close harmony with armour, to the benefit of both.

Consequently, a combined-arms doctrine (*Shiluv Kohot*) was developed, to allow for the successful deployment of mechanized infantry alongside armoured formations, supported by a greatly increased force of self-propelled artillery. Within this system the paratroopers would operate, like the other brigades, as mechanized infantry, but their particular skills would also see them provide a disproportionate number of men for the special counter-terror operations that would continue throughout the remainder of the decade.

Entebbe, 1976

The terrorist hijacking by the PFLP-EO group of Air France Flight 139 on 27 June 1976 set the stage for the most challenging and famous hostage rescue mission of the past 50 years. Landing at Entebbe airport in Uganda, the hijackers eventually kept 94 mainly Israeli hostages and the aircraft's 12-strong crew, threatening them all with execution if 53 imprisoned terrorists were not released from a number of jails. The stand-off at Entebbe was conducted with the acquiescence of the Ugandan dictator Idi Amin Dada, and the airport buildings were guarded externally by troops from the Ugandan Army.

The events of the Israeli rescue raid on 4 July are well known (see Osprey RAID 2 *Israel's Lightning Strike: the Raid on Entebbe 1976*), but despite its renowned success it should be appreciated that at the time of the mission's planning, attempts at hostage rescues were often bloody and unsuccessful. The grim examples of the Munich Olympics massacre in September 1972, and even more so that of the Ma'alot massacre in May 1974, were all too fresh in the memory. (At Ma'alot a school was taken over by three Palestinian terrorists from the DFLP, with 115 hostages, many of them schoolchildren.

Paratroopers and a Bell UH-1D 'Huey' search for Fatah terrorists in the Ramat Hasharon area in the wake of the attack on the Haifa-Tel Aviv highway on 11 March 1978. Known as the 'Coastal Road Massacre', this attack cost the lives of 38 Israelis (including 13 children) and wounded 71 more. The Israeli response came in the form of Operation *Litani*, a major incursion by the IDF into southern Lebanon in pursuit of PLO cells – a significant escalation of the long-running Israeli campaign against the troublesome Palestinian presence in that region. (GPO)

The attempt to free them three days later by *Sayeret Matkal* resulted in the terrorists killing 25 people, 22 of whom were children, and wounding 68 more.) In such an atmosphere the probable success of any attempt to mount a rescue of the Entebbe hostages was highly questionable, given that it had to be carried out far overseas and without any local support at all.

The raid involved about 100 personnel led by BrigGen Dan Shomron (a paratroop veteran who had started his military career in Bn 890 in 1955). The force for Operation *Thunderbolt* was made up of men from *Sayeret Matkal*; a hand-picked detachment of paratroopers from *Sayeret Tzanhanim*; and a selection of the best men from the Golani Brigade's *Sayeret* and its 1st *Barak* Battalion. The audacity of the plan was extraordinary: the whole rescue force would embark in four C-130 Hercules; fly across the Red Sea and into Africa while evading radar detection; land by night at a hostile airport guarded by an unknown number of enemy personnel; defeat the hijackers and any Ugandan soldiers who joined the fray; evacuate all the hostages – and be back in the air within an hour. The distances involved were unprecedented, and so were the risks; with so many interdependent 'moving parts' to the plan, the chances of something going catastrophically wrong were very high. In such circumstances it is remarkable that the operation was even authorized, and its success speaks to the obviously high level of competence displayed by all involved. One of the key advantages of such well-trained and experienced troops is their adaptability, being able to grasp the intricacies of a new operation quickly, and to adjust to unexpected changes without losing their coherence or their focus on the overall objective.

Operation *Litani*, 1978

Despite its success, unfortunately Entebbe was not to mark the end of ambitious terrorist 'spectaculars'. In early March 1978 an infiltration team from Fatah, a PLO faction, crossed the border from Lebanon, ending up hijacking a pair of buses on the Coastal Road from Tel Aviv to Haifa; the

Paratroopers parading in Ramat Gat, 1979. They are armed with the Galil ARM and wear the recently adopted 'Ephod' load-carrying system (already seen here in two slightly differing variants). This was a significant improvement on the old British-type canvas webbing equipment that had remained more or less unchanged from the War of Independence, and which would still be worn by some reservists and rear-echelon units well into the 1980s. (Yaacov Saar, GPO)

Paratroopers practicing a helicopter insertion during a training exercise in 1980. Such training was crucial in the development of a flexible and reactive force, but the immediate future would see the majority of paratroopers operating as armoured infantry in the hills of southern Lebanon, no differently from the IDF's other infantry brigades. (Moshe Milner, GPO)

affair ended in disaster, with 38 Israelis killed and 76 more wounded. Teams of paratroopers and Golani soldiers conducted hunts for the surviving terrorists, eventually bringing them all to book, but the provocation of the attack led to a major Israeli response. This was an invasion of southern Lebanon by 15,000 troops, up to the limit of the Litani River, in an attempt to bring the PLO and its associated factions to battle where it could defeat them for good. Since their eviction from Jordan the PLO had made a new home for themselves in Beirut and southern Lebanon, later exploiting that country's bloody and chaotic civil war which began in 1975. They had expanded and consolidated their power in the south of the country, developing a network of bases from which to launch attacks against northern Israel.

The invasion was never meant to be long-term, nor was it intended to interfere with local Lebanese politics (unlike its later 1982 iteration). 35 Paratroopers Brigade commanded by Col Yitzhak Mordechai, along with the Golani Bde and several armoured brigades, crossed the border on 14 March 1978. The regular battalions were mechanized, while *Sayeret Tzanhanim* operated from helicopters, engaging in pursuits reminiscent of those they had undertaken in the Jordan Valley during the War of Attrition. Despite some success (the paratroopers were credited with 40 per cent of the total 250 Palestinian fighters who were killed), the majority of the guerrillas retreated in the face of the Israeli advance, crossing the bridges over the Litani to the safety of the north. The PLO finally observed a UN ceasefire on 28 March, and the IDF withdrew in June. They left southern Lebanon to the care of the UN and local Christian and Shia militias friendly to Israel, but the Palestinians soon returned. Cross-border incursions would resume at an increasing level, eventually leading Israel to attempt to solve the problem once more, though on a far larger and more ambitious scale than before.

OPERATIONS, 1982–2005

The First Lebanon War, 1982

Launched on 6 June 1982, the conflict that would eventually be known as the First Lebanon War began with an Israeli invasion of southern Lebanon. Optimistically named Operation *Peace for Galilee*, its reported purpose was to drive the PLO training camps beyond striking distance of the Israeli border once and for all. In fact, the Israelis wanted the PLO gone from Lebanon entirely, including their centre of power in Beirut. It was hoped that the war would also break Syrian control of Lebanese politics, allowing an Israel-friendly government to come to power and thus securing Israel's northern border. Politically speaking, the ambition of the Israeli government (mostly of Prime Minister Menachem Begin and Minister of Defence Ariel Sharon) was breathtakingly unrealistic: the bitter factional hostilities tearing apart what had once been a delicately balanced multi-religious, multi-communal country since the outbreak of civil war in 1975 were far more complex than Israel appreciated.

Militarily, this would be the first major operation since *Litani* in 1978, and in scale it could only be compared with the Yom Kippur War of 1973. Three major IDF thrusts (task forces West, Centre and East) would cross the border and secure southern Lebanon, bottling up Beirut on the coast, and slamming the door on Syrian intervention from the Damascus road to the east. Task Force East (whose job was to secure the Bekaa Valley and the

First Lebanon War, 10 August 1982: paratroopers pause to discuss the best way to advance against a suspected terrorist hideout in the southern quarters of the Lebanese capital, Beirut, during Israel's Operation *Peace for Galilee*. At centre, note the altered shape of the new M76 Israeli helmet. (Yaakov Saar/GPO via Getty Images)

Paratroopers seen during house-to-house fighting in Beirut, August 1982. The tan-coloured haversack and canteen covers contrast with the olive-coloured rear pouch of the Ephod system. Later Ephods would have an integral haversack in matching green. (Yaakov Saar/GPO via Getty Images)

eastern slopes of the Hermon range) also included a 'Special Manoeuvre Force' led by BrigGen Yossi Peled which consisted of two brigades, one of infantry and the other of paratroopers, who had been specially trained and equipped in anti-tank warfare in anticipation of a Syrian Army armoured response.

Although there was now a much better balance between armour and infantry, as well as a better understanding of combined operations, the old IDF bias in favour of armour still played its part in the invasion. Despite some poor planning, tactical difficulties, and (more ominously) strategic confusion as to the ultimate goals of the war, overall the IDF's ability to achieve its objectives was still impressive. More extensive use was made of

A female weapons instructor examines an RPG round at a training camp, 1987. Captured in large numbers, until 1973 this weapon was available only to paratroop and commando units, but it later became general issue.

Women have always been liable for conscription, though for two years' service rather than for three. Despite their strong presence within the IDF for decades, before 2000 they were not permitted to serve in combat roles. Nevertheless, their supporting tasks in front-line units have often taken them into harm's way, and in the rear echelons many serve as expert weapons, parachute, and even tank-crew instructors. (Nati Harnik, GPO)

helicopter-borne troops, with the Israelis enjoying a more significant lift capacity than in previous wars, including 8 SA 321 Super Frelons, around 35 CH-53Ds, 2 S-65Cs, 29 Bell AB 206 Jet Rangers, 24 Augusta-Bell 212s, and 25 Bell Iroquois UH-lDs (Cordesman & Wagner 1990: 211). This airborne capability allowed paratroopers and other infantry the chance to regain some of the mobility they had lacked in the Yom Kippur War; successful landings outflanked enemy units on a number of occasions, though they were usually on a relatively small scale.

The local tactical failings of the IDF included some underestimation of their enemies – PLO, Syrian, and eventually Lebanese – as well as a lack of familiarity with much of the terrain in southern Lebanon, which was more mountainous and inhospitable than many commanders had anticipated. One notable exception to this short-sightedness was 35 Para Bde commanded by Col Yoram Yair, an officer well acquainted with the rigours of mountain warfare, who had taken considerable pains to ensure that his brigade was ready to fight in such terrain. During the early stages of the invasion Yair took Bn 50 from his brigade together with other infantry elements and supporting vehicles (over 400 in total) and embarked on an audacious naval landing – the largest amphibious operation in Israeli naval history – 40km south of Beirut. Landing at 1100hrs on 6 June 1982 at the mouth of the Awali River 3 miles north of Sidon, they leapfrogged the IDF's western thrust that had just taken Tyre further down the coast. Breaking out of the beachhead the following day, the landing force linked up with advancing ground forces and moved on into the city.

F WEST BANK, SOUTH LEBANON & GAZA, 2002–2009

(1) Light machine-gunner, Battalion 101; Nablus, 2002

A paratrooper from Bn 101's reconnaissance unit prepares to open fire with his Negev SF light machine gun during the battle of Nablus, a part of Operation *Defensive Shield* in April 2002. He wears a modern RBH-103 helmet, though it is mostly obscured by a *Mitznefet*, a baggy length of perforated cloth that is secured to the helmet's rim by an integral elasticated band; this comes in a woodland camouflage pattern that can be reversed to show a desert scheme. The Mitznefet's rather random and shapeless appearance, always differing from one man to another, is the point, since it obscures the outline of the wearer's helmet. Originally borrowing its name from an ancient item of Rabbinical headgear, the Mitznefet is more commonly called the 'clown hat' by those who wear it. His equipment includes a body-armour vest (issued since the 1970s in various forms, such 'flak vests' were locally made, though originally based on the American designs common during and soon after the Vietnam War), with a later-generation Ephod worn over it. This combination was being phased out from 2000 onwards in favour of the Advanced Ephod hybrid system that integrated the load-bearing vest with the body armour. He is armed with the 5.56mm Negev SF LMG, the feet of its bipod wrapped with cloth to cut down noise when grounding the weapon. Originally designed as a replacement for the unloved Galil ARM in the squad LMG role, this weapon was introduced in 1997 in two versions: the standard Negev with a 460mm barrel, and the Negev SF (special forces or 'commando' model) with a 330mm barrel. The gun suffered from teething troubles, but through a process of constant feedback and refinement it gradually became a much more effective weapon. The version shown here is the SF model, which was initially reserved for specialist units, though distribution to other front-line formations subsequently became more common. In 2012 the Negev NG-7 was introduced; built around the same operating system but chambered for 7.62x51mm NATO, it became the IDF's replacement for the FN MAG 58 General Purpose Machine Gun.

(2) 'Door-breacher', 551 Paratroopers Brigade; Lebanon, 2006

This reservist called up for service in the Second Lebanon War has just loaded a SIMON RLEM (Rifle Launched Entry Munition) onto his M4 carbine in preparation for his squad to breach a barricaded doorway in the town of Reshef, 2006. He is protected by his RBH-103 helmet, a pair of Gentex EPS-21 goggles (standard issue since the late 1990s), and his heavy second-generation Advanced Ephod body armour (the even more cumbersome first pattern had a pair of frontal 'tassets' for groin protection, as well as shoulder guards). This hybrid armour/load-carrying system offered good protection but proved to be heavy and restrictive, and was discontinued in 2006 in favour of lighter and more modular plate-carrier/vest combinations. He is armed with an M4 assault rifle fitted with an Aimpoint M4 sight; the M4 (and M4A1) had by this time become ubiquitous in Israeli service, though the use of the M16 platform, particularly among specialist units, went back to the early 1970s when the US supplied M16A1 and CAR-15 rifles. The SIMON door-breaching munition, developed by Rafael Systems, is launched by attaching it to the muzzle and firing a standard 5.56mm round; the bullet is caught in a shot-trap, in turn propelling the SIMON for up to 30m. The 40cm stand-off rod, the munition's most obvious feature, impacts the door to be breached and detonates the warhead at its base; this creates a blast wave that covers a much larger area, and which will knock even armoured doors off their hinges. The SIMON also proved to be very popular with US troops in the urban combat environments of Iraq (the US Army designated it as the M100 Grenade Rifle Entry Munition, GREM).

(3) MATADOR operator, 35 Paratroopers Brigade; Operation *Cast Lead*, Gaza, 2009

The soldier's personal weapon, an M4A1 fitted with an ACOG (Advanced Combat Optical Gunsight) 1×32 Red Dot Scope, is carried slung ready to hand (so mostly hidden here). The 90mm MATADOR (Man-portable Anti-Tank, Anti-Door), colloquially known to Israelis as the 'nutcracker', allows the user to engage both armoured vehicles and structures. First seeing service with the IDF in the January 2009 Gaza War, the MATADOR is a disposable weapon that delivers its HEAT (High Explosive Anti-Tank)/HESH (High Explosive Squash Head) warhead out to a maximum of 500m. Both anti-armour and anti-structure capabilities exist within the same warhead: fired 'as is', the rocket will act as a HESH round to breach walls and destroy strongpoints, but the nosecone contains an integral 'probe' that, when extended by the user, transforms it into an effective HEAT projectile capable of penetrating up to 500mm of armour.

7 May 2001: a paratrooper uses the telescopic sight on his M16A2 to scan the surrounding area for Palestinian insurgents as he mans a new army outpost in Israeli-controlled territory on the outskirts of the Palestinian West Bank town of Beit Jala. The IDF set up the outpost in an area that was the scene of violent gun battles the previous day, establishing themselves on a hilltop that overlooked the main bypass road between Jerusalem and the southern West Bank. Note the stuffed haversack and lower rear pouch on his Ephod gear. (Photo by David Silverman/Newsmakers)

The mission of Yair's paratroopers was to clear Sidon of PLO fighters, a difficult and dangerous task in the face of stiff resistance. A routine was developed: suppress snipers with artillery and air strikes, enter the targeted building, mop up, exit, rest, regroup, and repeat – on and on, until the city was cleared. Once Sidon was secured by 9 June the paratroopers moved off north into the mountains, where they secured passes and pacified PLO strongholds, ensuring a clear passage for the following armoured units. Eventually they managed to break through the Syrian defensive line outside Beirut itself, linking up with allied Christian-Lebanese militias to the north of the city. Even if the war in general was dominated by mechanized and armoured forces using the weight of superior firepower to batter their way to victory, in this instance the value of well-trained, tough, adaptable infantry who had the stamina to operate effectively in different environments was amply demonstrated.

The major fighting was over by the middle of September 1982, giving way to a drawn-out period during which the initial Israeli miscalculations about the political and strategic realities of Lebanon became ever more apparent. The ostensible goal – the removal of the PLO – was achieved, but the supposed political benefits that some had expected to reap from their bolstering of the Christian and Druze factions never materialized. The IDF presence dragged on for three more years, alienating the local population and doing much to encourage the growth of the nascent Hezbollah. This Iranian-backed Shia militia would come to dominate southern Lebanon in a way that the PLO never had, denying Galilee the security that had been the war's stated aim.

Counter-insurgency and occupation

The conflict in Lebanon did not end with the withdrawal of major IDF units in 1985. Given the danger still posed by insurgent forces including groups such as Amal and Hezbollah, the IDF occupied a 'security zone' that stretched from the Israeli border northwards to the Litani River, providing support for the allied (Christian-dominated) South Lebanon Army who were nominally in charge of the whole area. A series of outposts were established throughout the region, manned by IDF regulars and reservists from all the infantry brigades (including the paratroopers) on a rotational basis.

As an institution the IDF had to develop in three important ways in the years following the First Lebanon War. First and most importantly, the nature of the conflicts in which they were engaged had changed radically from the past. Israel's military doctrine had evolved in a rather haphazard way, but at its core it relied on aggression, creative thinking, speed and manoeuvre. It always had to take the fight to the enemy and do battle on his ground, not Israel's, since the small country has very little in the way of strategic depth to exploit. After the first few months of the First Lebanon War there would be no military operations on a commensurate scale until they invaded again in 2006. The intervening years were dominated by occupation duties in South Lebanon and policing actions in the West Bank and Gaza Strip, mostly in response to the 'first' and 'second' *intifadas* (popular uprisings). Conflicts were now asymmetric: long-lasting, low-intensity fighting against decentralized guerrilla groups whose prime

Paratroopers light candles for the Jewish festival of Hanukkah in their outpost overlooking the West Bank Palestinian town of Nablus, 21 December 2003. As always in such situations, the troops who had to man such outposts in the occupied territories or during the long campaign in southern Lebanon often found the routine crushingly boring, sapping morale and making it difficult to remain as alert as they needed to be. This rendered them more vulnerable to the occasional but usually well-planned attacks or attempted kidnappings by Hamas or Hezbollah. (IDF/Getty Images)

tactics were the rocket attack and the ambush, or the pacification of discontented civilian populations supported by the likes of Hamas and other non-state actors. Such 'warfare', if it could even be termed as such, could not be fought in the traditional manner, and would force doctrinal and tactical change on the paratroopers and other infantry brigades who would bear the brunt of such duties.

Secondly, there was a growing appreciation of the benefits that new technology could bring, particularly the value of precision strikes from the air, and this led to a gradual preference for 'stand-off' engagements as opposed to the more traditional ground-led operations. In a country as small as Israel there had always been an awareness of the cost of war, and while the move away from full-scale conflicts reduced the numbers of dead and wounded, those that were killed lost their lives during occupation or policing duties that were harder to justify to an increasingly querulous domestic audience. It was therefore natural to invest in new systems and technologies that reduced the exposure of ground troops to enemy action.

Thirdly, the absence of a well-defined doctrine from earlier years was addressed through the 1990s, but the results would prove to be less than satisfactory. A culture of managerialism developed that saw a growing distance between the army's senior leadership and its fighting elements – a radical departure from what had been one of the IDF's defining characteristics in its early years. The famous cry of 'Follow me!' was gradually drowned out by a series of new, acronym-heavy systems and processes that were meant to make the IDF into a thoroughly modern war-fighting machine. In fact, it became a top-heavy organization wedded to overly complex 'methodologies', which could not stand up to the rigours of a high-intensity engagement (as would be rudely demonstrated during the 33-day Second Lebanon War in 2006).

A paratrooper armed with an M4 fitted with an Israeli-made Elbit Falcon Mk I optical 'red dot' gun sight, photographed during an IDF operation against Palestinian fighters in Beit Jala, 2001. The provision of non-magnifying reflector ('reflex') sights became much more common in the 1990s, with the IDF officially adopting the Elbit Falcon in 1997. Such sights make acquiring and hitting a target much easier, but many of them cost as much as or more than the rifle to which they are fitted. (Avi Ohayon, GPO)

OPPOSITE
18 April 2002, Jenin: paratroopers with some of the weapons (M16/M16A1 rifles, ammunition and mortar rounds) found during the fighting against Palestinian militants in the West Bank. The soldier on the left wears a first-generation Advanced Ephod, a rather unwieldy hybrid combination of body-armour vest with load-carrying harness first issued in 2000. (IDF/Getty Images)

An exhausted-looking paratrooper having a smoke, photographed at the Israeli border village of Avivim on 29 July 2006. He and his comrades have just arrived back from seven days of intense combat with Hezbollah guerrillas in the southern Lebanese village of Bint Jbeil. His Ephod load-carrying gear is likely to have an integrated armour-plate carrier. He is armed with some variant of the M4 carbine, and carries a personal radio – probably a PRC-148 – with a blade antenna. (Christopher Furlong/ Getty Images)

The period of drawn-out low-intensity engagements that followed the IDF withdrawal from Lebanon was punctuated by more significant operations with limited goals, usually lasting no more than a few days or weeks. The Second Intifada had erupted in 2000, requiring the units newly returned from Lebanon to adjust their focus to the Gaza Strip and the West Bank. The IDF engaged in notable operations in 2002 around Nablus (Operation *Defensive Shield*), and in mid-November that year in Hebron, which the IDF occupied in reaction to the killing of 12 Israelis and the wounding of

14 others (most of them members of the security forces or civilian security guards escorting Jewish worshippers). In 2004 a push was mounted into the Gaza Strip to try to destroy tunnel networks (Operation *Rainbow*). The same year saw raids in search of Hamas rockets, on Beit Hanoun in northern Gaza (Operations *Forward Shield* and *Days of Penitence*). The results achieved by such operations were local and mostly temporary, dealing with symptoms rather than causes.

Such conflicts encouraged static and reactive tactics, and were particularly difficult for elite infantry such as the paratroopers, whose defining ethos was diametrically opposed to such 'passive' engagement with the enemy. Neither did it help that in the West Bank and the Gaza Strip the difference between fully paid-up insurgents and often justifiably angry civilians was far from obvious. The aggressiveness of elite IDF units did not lessen, however, and this period saw an increase in the (already substantial) role played by Israeli special forces, including the *sayerot* of the various paratroopers' brigades. New small-unit tactics were developed to deal with the realities of fighting in densely built-up civilian areas. There was increased reliance on localized intelligence (including real-time situational awareness provided by hand-launched drones); objectives were more tightly focused, and the value of artillery and armour support in covering advances and withdrawals was exploited.

One such innovation came about during the battle of Nablus (fought in April 2002 as part of Operation *Defensive Shield*), driven by the lateral thinking of Col Aviv Kokhavi at the head of 35 Paratroopers Brigade. He recognized that the dense maze of alleyways, doors and windows that awaited his men offered the defenders a wealth of opportunities to establish

A group of soldiers from Para Bn 101 photographed on their return from battle against Hezbollah in Bint Jbeil, 29 July 2006. Back in southern Lebanon three days later, on 1 August, 22-year-old *Samal rishon* (1st Sgt) Yehonatan Einhorn (pictured left) was one of three Israeli soldiers killed in fierce fighting against Hezbollah in the area of Aita al-Shaab. (Christopher Furlong/ Getty Images)

Paratroopers mourn at the grave of their comrade-in-arms Lt Ilan Gabay during his funeral on 2 August 2006 in the northern Israeli town of Kiryat Tivon. Gabay, aged 21, was one of the three soldiers killed in action against Hezbollah near Aita al-Shaab the previous day. On the Class A uniform, note (right) the shoulder tab of 35 Paratroopers Brigade (see Plate E1). (David Silverman/ Getty Images)

ambushes, killing-zones and booby traps, and he refused to engage with the battlespace as it was. Instead he ordered his troops to blow new pathways through walls so that they could move from room to room and house to house without exposing themselves to the potential deathtrap of the streets. These classic World War II tactics, originally perfected in North West Europe in 1944–45, proved successful. Employed in subsequent actions in built-up areas, they probably also encouraged the adoption of the 90mm MATADOR 'nutcracker' shoulder-launched rocket, introduced in 2009, which can be used against armour but is also highly effective at blowing man-sized holes in walls.

G *GADSAR TZANHANIM, 2012*
(1 & 2) ATGM team, Reconnaissance Battalion 5135, 2012
An anti-tank guided missile team from the 5174th Anti-Tank Company (a sub-unit of Recon Bn 5135 'Horned Viper' within 35 Para Bde) prepare to use their Spike MR – known as the 'Gil' in IDF service – in a live fire exercise. The gunner **(1)** sits cross-legged, focusing all his attention on the missile's fire control unit. The assistant/loader **(2)** approaches carrying two spare missiles, one in a harness on his back, the other in his hand; his personal weapon is an M4A1 rifle fitted with a Meprolight Mepro 21 sight. Both paratroopers wear the RBH-103 helmet, standard olive-green fatigues, kneepads, jump boots, and late-model Ephod equipment.

The system they are using, the Spike MR (Medium Range), is a man-portable and platform-adaptable missile system that can engage targets at ranges between 200 and 2,500m. The system (comprising the fire control unit, battery, tripod and thermal sight) weighs a total of 13kg and can be broken down or assembled within 30 seconds. Each missile in its disposable housing weighs 14kg, and spare rounds are carried in a special back harness. The Spike MR uses an electro-optical CCD/IIR seeker and delivers a tandem HEAT warhead designed to defeat reactive armour. There is a smaller shoulder-launched version known as the Spike SR that fires an 8kg missile out to a maximum of 1,500m, as well as two longer-range versions, the LR and LR II. The LR has a range of 4,000m; it is due to be superseded during 2018 by the LR II, with a range extended to 5,500m.

Paratroopers from 55 Para Bde (Reserve) dance before their deployment in Operation *Change of Direction 11*. This last Israeli offensive of the Second Lebanon War was launched on 11 August 2006, coming to an end three days later with the imposition of a UN ceasefire. Paratroopers from both 55 and the regular 35 Bde were inserted by helicopter into the central zone near the villages of Kafra and Yatar, but their engagements would prove to be as confused, inconclusive and disappointing as those endured by the rest of the IDF. (Moshe Miner, GPO)

OPERATIONS, 2006–2014

The Second Lebanon War, 2006

The nominal cause of the war was the killing of three IDF soldiers and the kidnap of two others in a Hezbollah border raid on 12 July 2006. The Israeli response aimed to find the kidnapped soldiers during a larger operation that would destroy Hezbollah as a force in southern Lebanon – a highly ambitious goal that many thought unrealistic from the outset. The core of the attack would be conducted by the IAF, in the belief that a sufficient degradation of Hezbollah's infrastructure and leadership could be achieved by air power alone to force them to withdraw (Farquhar 2009: 13–14).

There was a belief in Hezbollah, borne out to some degree by the IDF's long retreat from Lebanon from 1985 to 2000, that Israel lacked the will to prosecute a full-scale ground war, instead preferring to rely on artillery and air power to overmaster its opponents. Hezbollah had developed layers of missile batteries that stretched from the Israeli border all the way back past the Litani towards Beirut. They had also developed doctrine for the storing and launch of their weapons (estimated at somewhere between 9,000 and 13,000 rockets, mostly supplied by Syria and Iran); this hid them from Israeli surveillance, and allowed a team to come together, launch a missile,

and then disperse before the IDF's air and artillery assets could respond to it. Hezbollah's defensive system consisted of decentralized guerrilla units connected by a network of underground bunkers and tunnel systems that ran all the way back beyond the Litani. Such fighters (either independent of, or integral to the rocket batteries they supported) relied on booby traps, mines, a mix of advanced light weapons and specially trained anti-tank units to bear the brunt of any possible Israeli invasion attempt. They had at least 9,000 men under arms, made up of professionally trained commando forces supplemented by battle-tested militias filled with many veterans of the 18-year conflict that had concluded with Israel's withdrawal in 2000.

The first few days of the war showed up the shortcomings of the air campaign, making a ground assault necessary if the IDF was to have any chance of achieving its operational goals. The initial reports back from Maroun al-Ras, site of the first foray across the border, were discouraging: resistance was far stronger and better prepared than the Israelis had expected, and IDF armour was encountering significant AT activity. Reinforcements in the shape of Bn 101 from 35 Para Bde were sent in, but the long and grinding years of counter-insurgency had degraded many of the basic skills needed to conduct high-intensity operations effectively; failures were seen at the platoon level and above, including among officers. Reserves were called up to try to recover the situation, but the process was something of a shambles; even at the height of the IDF's advance, with

10 December 2009: a paratroop *segen* (first lieutenant – note two green bars printed on khaki shoulder-strap slide) acts as his own radio operator as his brigade completes a week-long live-fire training exercise on the Golan Heights. (David Silverman/Getty Images)

over 10,000 troops in-country, they barely managed to penetrate 4 miles beyond the border.

The Israeli experience of asymmetric warfare over the preceding decades had also changed perceptions among some senior planners and members of the General Staff, causing several of them to question the parameters of victory and loss in such conflicts. Long-term conflicts waged against non-state actors in an ongoing series of low-intensity encounters rarely, if ever, led to the sort of successes that characterized the battles of the 1967, 1973 and 1982 wars. In a communications-rich modern world the mere appearance of success could be as important (and significantly easier to achieve) than actual success. One event, the entry of a team from 35 Para Bde into the Lebanese border town of Bint Jbeil for the purpose of raising an Israeli flag over the former IDF HQ building, is representative of such an approach. The town was not taken, but the media benefits of symbolically 'capturing' it would be more or less the same as if Bint Jbeil had actually

H

OPERATION *PROTECTIVE EDGE*; GAZA, JULY–AUGUST 2014

(1) Paratrooper, 35 Paratroopers Brigade

Rushing into a dust-choked alleyway during the street-fighting in Gaza, he is intent on reaching cover. On his helmet are a pair of covered goggles and a *Mitznefet* 'clown hat'. He carries his magazines, medical kit and other necessities in his Ephod – an Israeli-made Marom-Dolphin TV 7711 – worn over a Hashmonai Level III body-armour vest. The range of variations found among Ephods, vests and plate-carriers is enormous, with items of differing styles and capacities from various manufacturers used side by side (especially in reservist units). This situation is further complicated by the preferences of individual units and soldiers, who may adapt or rig up their own configurations as they see fit. He is armed with an X95 carbine (also known as the Micro-Tavor or MTAR), fitted with a Mepro 21 sight and a dedicated flashlight. Developed from the Tavor family of assault rifles that were trialled by the IDF through 2001–2002, the X95 carbine is only 580mm (22.8in) long but still has a 330mm (13in) barrel due to its bullpup configuration. Fed from 30-round steel or polymer box magazine and weighing 3.3kg unloaded, it is closer in size to a personal defence weapon than an assault rifle, but still fires the 5.56x45mm NATO round; this makes it very useful in close combat in built-up areas, a regular feature of IDF encounters in the seemingly endless low-intensity skirmishing in the occupied territories. It is effective out to 300m, more than sufficient for urban warfare; can be adapted for left- or right-handed use; and comes with the integral Picatinny rails that are a necessity for modern modular firearm systems. As of 2009, the X95 was selected to become the standard issue weapon throughout much of the IDF, with the re-equipping of entire infantry brigades expected to be complete by the end of 2018. The sight used in this instance is the Mepro 21, a fairly ubiquitous attachment on IDF assault rifles and carbines. Developed by the Israeli company Meprolight in conjunction with IDF special forces, it is a reflex sight designed for close-quarter combat, allowing the user to keep both eyes open for rapid target acquisition.

(2) Grenadier, 35 Paratroopers Brigade

The grenadier carries the 5.56mm X95 419 (so called from its 419mm/16.5in barrel) with an underslung integrated IWI GL 40 grenade launcher; the X95 can also mount the M203 in the same role. The launcher takes 40x46mm grenade rounds, has a 303mm (12in) barrel, and adds 1.3kg to the weight of the carbine. The GL 40 is effective out to 150m with a maximum range of 400m, and can fire a range of rounds including high explosive, HEDP (High-Explosive Dual Purpose – anti-armour plus anti-personnel), illumination, marker, and CS gas. His weapon is also fitted with a Mepro 21 index sight as well as a Mepro GLS (Grenade Launcher Sight), a compact self-illuminated unit that is adjustable for both windage and elevation, and which can be mounted directly on the 419's Picatinny top rail or behind the Mepro 21, as is the case here.

(3) *Sayeret Tzanhanim* operator, 35 Paratroopers Brigade

Tasked with the most difficult, dangerous and sensitive work, the men of the *sayeret tzanhanim* special recon units are among the best-trained troops in the IDF. The type of operations they are expected to conduct means that a broader range of weaponry and equipment are made available to them, leading to greater variety and personalization than would typically be found in a normal infantry battalion. This operator advances with measured caution, his rifle held in a safe position but ready to be brought to bear immediately if required. His balaclava and sunglasses are as much to avoid the muck and dust of the streets as to conceal his identity. His helmet is standard issue, but has an ITT VIP (Visual Identification Projector) fixed to its rear edge; this can display infra-red or white light, marking his position in order to reduce the risk of 'friendly-fire mishaps' during the inevitable uncertainties of night fighting. His Ephod is probably one that he has personally adapted to his operational needs, and his choice of personal weapon is the tried and tested M4A1. This example has had its forestock replaced with an aluminium ARMS SIR rail system providing four Picatinny rails for attachments at 3, 6, 9, and 12 o'clock, allowing a pistol foregrip to be added. The main optic is a Trijicon ACOG 4x32 sight, and an Insight Technology AN/PEQ-15 (which provides infrared and visible-aim lasers, as well as an infrared illuminator) has been fixed to the front right section of the forestock. He also wears on his thigh a 'drop-holster' for his back-up weapon, a 9x19mm Glock 19 with a 17-round magazine.

A pair of paratroopers photographed during a lull in fighting against Hamas militants in the Gaza Strip, 10 January 2009, allowing a view of their small arms. At right is a 5.56mm CTAR-21 carbine – with a barrel length of only 380mm it was a more popular variant of the longer Tavor TAR-21, but 2009 would see the launch of the even shorter MTAR-21 (also known as the Micro-Tavor or X95), a carbine with a 330mm barrel that is set to become the standard-issue weapon throughout much of the IDF during 2018. His companion to the left carries the GTAR-21, a longer-barrelled version of the Tavor that allows the addition of an M203 40mm under-slung grenade launcher. Both weapons allow the attachment of modular elements such as lights and a variety of optics; nearly all personal weapons are issued with a magnifying and/or reflex sight, depending on the anticipated role. (IDF via Getty Images)

fallen to the IDF. As such a potentially costly endeavour would have little long-term tactical value, the illusory version would serve just as well as the real thing (Kober 2016: 80-81). It is arguable how realistic such a cynical approach can be: for the 'underdog' a propaganda coup has obvious value, but even for a group like Hezbollah (never mind a state like Israel), claims of success must have a degree of substance if the integrity of an operation or even a war is to be maintained.

The imminent UN ceasefire caused a last-minute scramble to rescue something from the mess, resulting in Operation *Change of Direction 11*, initiated on 11 August 2006, three days before the ceasefire. The plan would have been ambitious even without the disappointing performance of the IDF over the preceding weeks. It called for the airlifting of part of 98 'Fire Brigade' Div to a sector just south of the Litani River, linking up with other IDF divisions to encircle more or less the whole of southern Lebanon. In the event, the actions undertaken were far less impressive in scope, with poor planning and incoherent objectives making the whole affair a fitting capstone to the folly that had preceded it. Colonel Hagai Mordechai's entire 35 Para Bde was meant to be airlifted to the Bmaryamin plain, but when one of the helicopters was shot down during the first drop the IDF called off further flights, leaving Mordechai and 200 paratroopers sitting at the landing zone, their mission postponed again and again until the ceasefire came into effect on 14 August.

Operation *Cast Lead*, 2009
Significant changes were instigated after the debacle of the Second Lebanon War, with renewed emphasis on training, leadership and tactical proficiency

which went some way to renew the IDF's sense of pride in itself. Perhaps inevitably, a 2008 campaign of rocket attacks by Hamas in the Gaza Strip would provide the opportunity to test how seriously such changes had been adopted. There had already been a short engagement in Gaza in June 2006 prior to the invasion of Lebanon; known as Operation *Summer Rains*, its aim was the rescue of a kidnapped soldier and the suppression of Palestinian rocket attacks. This was followed by Operation *Autumn Clouds* in November 2006, but neither of these incursions had approached the scope (or the subsequent disappointment) of the Lebanon invasion, since the Palestinians were a far less potent threat than Hezbollah.

The ground phase of Operation *Cast Lead* started on 3 January 2009 and was led by 35 Para Bde in concert with the Givati and Golani Bdes, against an estimated 15,000 Hamas fighters. The paratroopers operated in the northern end of the Strip, moving towards Atatra; they were led by armoured bulldozers, with helicopter gunships providing air cover and drones supplying real-time intelligence. Operations were usually conducted in darkness to make the most of the IDF's night-imaging equipment. Combined-arms teams of tanks supported by infantry, engineers and bomb-sniffer dogs followed the paths of Caterpillar D-9 bulldozers that smashed their way through buildings, to make new roads rather than trusting to the existing network that was almost certainly heavily mined.

Hamas was unprepared for the strength and intensity of the Israeli ground attack. The Israeli advance shattered its rudimentary communications network, reducing its commanders' ability to control their men. Many of these decided that discretion was the better part of valour in such circumstances, abandoning their positions and melting away into the civilian population.

An officer briefs his paratroopers on an operation to hunt for Hamas tunnels in Gaza, 2014. Such work proved to be difficult and dangerous, in no small part due to the fact that Hamas fighters understood the goals of the Israeli incursion and planned effective countermeasures – booby traps and ambushes – to hamper the paratroopers. (CC BY 2.0)

Sunrise in northern Israel, during a paratroop brigade exercise in 2003. (IDF/Getty Images)

Hamas tried to avoid pitched battles as determinedly as the IDF sought them out, but the pressure applied by the Israelis was inexorable, and the Hamas losses mounted. The IDF infantry brigades managed to apply precision fire, and the manoeuvring of combined-arms teams ensured that successes were exploited effectively and quickly. Such flexibility was enhanced by the decision to allow key assets previously held at divisional level to be employed by brigade commanders as they saw fit – UAVs, attack helicopters and air sorties were all added to a commander's toolkit, allowing a faster and more hard-hitting response to developments on the battlefield. By the time Israel called a unilateral ceasefire on 18 January there was no doubt about which side had won.

Operation *Protective Edge*, 2014

Precipitated by the kidnap and murder of three Jewish teenagers by a Hamas terror cell and the subsequent Israeli search for the perpetrators, another short, sharp campaign in Gaza began on 8 July 2014, once again with the objective of eliminating Hamas' rocket capability as well as destroying the network of tunnels that supported it. Such actions have been termed 'mowing the grass' – in effect, operations to reduce the enemy's capability to a more manageable level, at least for a while. In the now familiar pattern, a series of intensive air and artillery strikes were unleashed, followed on 17 July by a ground assault that would last for three weeks.

The fighting proved to be more intense that that experienced during *Cast Lead*, in part because the resolve of many Hamas fighters now seemed stiffer, and also because they had better tools at their disposal. One IDF senior intelligence officer noted that while Hamas tactics had not evolved in recent years, the same could not be said for its weaponry; this now included the

Russian-made RPG-29 that was specially designed for urban warfare, as well as a range of modern anti-tank weapons that featured consistently in Hamas attacks on IDF units.

Some teams from the *Gadsar Tzanhanim* of 35 Para Bde were drafted in specifically to hunt for tunnels, a difficult task that often ended in sharp firefights. One squad found itself battling insurgents who had burst out from the mouth of a tunnel while they were simultaneously ambushed from the windows of the surrounding houses; the entire squad were wounded and one man killed. In spite of such dangers, the rewards for finding and securing a tunnel could be significant, with many large stockpiles of weapons and equipment found in the course of such searches. The tunnel teams were supported by tanks, as well as snipers who would take up position in nearby houses, establishing protective fields of fire. The now well-established habit of blowing holes through walls rather than trusting to potentially booby-trapped doors was often seen, but the range of IEDs encountered was extensive, and not all of them could be avoided. One paratroop commander noted that entire streets were covered with wires connected to IEDs, and engineers with bomb-sniffing dogs proved invaluable on more than one occasion.

For the IDF the immediate lessons of this short, intense operation validated existing combined-arms tactics for infantry and armour in both rural and urban environments, though there were areas that invited improvement. For some paratroopers, their experiences during *Protective Edge* reinforced the need to attend to basic skills like the immediate application of first aid, as well as personal proficiency in combat. The asymmetric nature of many of the IDF's encounters showed that conventional reliance on a 'battle line' was ineffective; the fractured and dispersed nature of urban fighting demanded that the individual soldier be able to meet and defeat his enemy on a one-to-one basis. Such combats were often conducted at close quarters, where proficiency with small arms and in squad tactics were determining factors. In addition, it was observed that though teaching troops how to operate in urban (and even subterranean) environments was an obvious requirement, it was one that should be built on the time-tested basics of field tactics rather than substituted for them. Finally, it was observed that the old approach to leadership ('Follow Me!') had started to reappear during *Cast Lead* and was evident during *Protective Edge* – as reflected in increased casualty figures among commanders. The renewed sense of responsibility had translated into faster decision-making that was also better informed, because the officers, from brigade level down, were more often than not closer to the heart of the fight.

CONCLUSION

The lands that surround Israel have rarely been in such a state of uncertainty as they are today. Not since the Yom Kippur War has regional instability been so marked, primarily as a result of the catastrophic consequences of the Coalition misadventure in Iraq, and the implosion of Syria in the wake of the abortive 'Arab Spring'. Such geopolitical contortions are exacerbated by the growing regional rivalry between Saudi Arabia and Iran, the interference of external actors such as Russia and Turkey, and the general instability of Libya, Yemen and several other North African and Levantine states. The traditional role of Egypt as the centre of regional Arabic leadership seems somewhat diminished in the wake of three successive governments in as many years.

Aluf mishne Ofer Winter of the Givati Brigade makes his way through a cramped but impressively well-constructed Hamas tunnel in the Gaza Strip, 2014. Though the ostensible reason for Operation *Protective Edge* was retaliation for the kidnapping and murder of three Israeli teenagers, a significant element of the ground campaign was the need to find and destroy as many tunnels as possible. At least 34 were eradicated in the course of just under four weeks. (Zach Haim, GPO)

OPPOSITE
Soldiers all carrying the IWI X95 'Micro-Tavor' carbine during Operation *Brother's Keeper* in Judea and Samaria, June 2014; no two of them are mounting the same optic. From left to right, those in the foreground are a Mepro RDS Pro red-dot sight, a Mepro Mor reflex sight with integrated laser pointers, and an ACOG. The orange 'buttons' just visible protruding from the ejection ports of the carbines are simple angled plastic dowels, commonly called 'chamber flags', that plug into the weapon's breech, ensuring that live rounds cannot be chambered accidentally. (CC BY 2.0)

A paratrooper in the mouth of a recently uncovered Palestinian tunnel during Operation *Protective Edge*, 20 July 2014. The full extent of the tunnel network beneath Gaza is difficult to determine, though it was (and probably still is) extensive, running for dozens of miles and connecting many of the main centres of population in the Gaza Strip. For Israelis the fact that at least 14 of the tunnels were found to have crossed the border was a source of significant concern. Aside from the access that such a network allowed, tunnels were a safe haven from IDF surveillance or airstrikes, and provided secure storage for supplies, small arms, and Hamas's large arsenal of rockets. (CC BY 2.0)

For Israel the situation is not as overtly threatening as during the first decades of its existence; the relatively stable borders with Egypt and Jordan allow some peace of mind, but the situation in Syria is of grave concern. The outcome of that civil war is yet to be determined, but it has already seen an increase in the military reach of Iran, as well as providing significant combat experience for Hezbollah. With the opportunity to engage in high-intensity

Paratroopers operating in Gaza, 2014. The ground element of *Protective Edge* lasted from 8 July to 5 August, with a ceasefire coming into effect on 26 August. This brief war had cost the IDF 67 lives; losses among the Palestinians are more difficult to judge, with somewhere in the region of 700–900 militants and 740–1,600 civilians being killed. (CC BY 2.0)

combat using larger formations that would normally be seen in southern Lebanon, as well as assaulting towns and cities in complex and ambitious operations, Hezbollah has most likely enjoyed a significant increase in its war-fighting capability. Such evolutions in tactical and organisational skill are an obvious cause of concern for IDF officers who have to plan for possible conflicts in the near future. With an ascendant Iran, and perhaps weakening support from traditional Western allies, there is a chance that future regional conflicts may move away from the asymmetric pattern that has been the norm for the IDF since the mid-1970s; some in the Israeli General Staff are giving serious consideration to the possibility of a resurgence of large-scale conventional warfare. The Paratroopers Brigade is undertaking new training programmes that will see brigade-level air-dropped insertions carried out and supported on an unprecedented scale – an acknowledgement that the strategic capability offered by airborne forces is worth maintaining in such uncertain times.

The challenges faced by the IDF's paratroopers are not all external. Domestic politics, which one might charitably describe as 'lively', will always play their part, as will the changing demographics of an evolving nation. The national relationship with the armed forces is different from that during Israel's early wars of survival. Service in the IDF is no longer seen as synonymous with citizenship in the way that it once was, and the current model of universal conscription may well evolve into a more European model in the not too distant future. Trust in the nation's political and military leaders to exercise power only in the best interests of the state has also been damaged by the tortuous misadventures in Lebanon, and the sometimes ugly realities of waging long-term, low-intensity wars among neighbouring populations.

Amid such uncertainties, the need to maintain a force that has the skill, training and reserves of manpower to engage in a range of combat scenarios against state and non-state actors remains undiminished, and the IDF's paratroopers have long come to define just such a capability.

SELECT BIBLIOGRAPHY

Achcar, Gilbert & Warsahawski, Michel, *The 33 Day War: Israel's War on Hezbollah in Lebanon and Its Aftermath* (London: SAQI, 2007)

Cohen, Stuart, *Israel and Its Army: From Cohesion to Confusion* (Oxford: Routledge, 2008)

Cordesman, Anthony H., *Arab-Israeli Military Forces in an Era of Asymmetric Wars* (Westport, CT: Praeger Security International, 2006)

Creveld, Martin van, *The Sword and the Olive: A Critical History of the Israeli Defense Force* (New York, NY: Public Affairs, 2002)

Creveld, Martin van, 'Israel's Lebanese War: A Preliminary Assessment' in *RUSI Journal, 151:5 (2006)* pp. 40–43

Eilam, Ehud, *Israel's Way of War: A Strategic and Operational Analysis, 1948–2014* (Jefferson, NC: McFarland & Co., 2015)

Farquhar, Scott C., *Back to Basics: A Study of the Second Lebanon War and Operation CAST LEAD* (Fort Leavenworth, KS: Combat Studies Institute Press, 2009)

Friedman, Matti, *Pumpkinflowers: A Soldier's Story of a Forgotten War* (London: Biteback, 2016)

Grassiani, Erella, *Soldiering Under Occupation: Processes of Numbing among Israeli Soldiers in the Al-Aqsa Intifada* (New York, NY: Berghahn Books, 2013)

Handel, Michael I., 'The Evolution of Israeli Strategy: The Psychology of Insecurity and the Quest for Absolute Security', in Williamson Murray ed., et al., *The Making of Strategy: Rulers, States, and War* (Cambridge: Cambridge University Press, 1994) pp. 534–578

Harel, Amos & Issacharoff, Avi, *34 Days: Israel, Hezbollah, and the War in Lebanon* (Basingstoke: Palgrave Macmillan, 2008)

Katz, Samuel M., *Israeli Defence Forces since 1973*, Elite 8 (Oxford: Osprey, 1986)

Katz, Samuel M., *Follow Me!: A History of Israel's Military Elite* (London: Arms & Armour Press, 1989)

Kober, Avi, 'The Rise and Fall of Israeli Operational Art, 1948–2008' in *The Evolution of Operational Art: From Napoleon to the Present*, John Andreas Olsen & Martin van Creveld eds (Oxford: Oxford University Press. 2011) pp. 166–194

Kober, Avi, *Practical Soldiers: Israel's Military Thought and Its Formative Factors* (Leiden, Netherlands: Brill, 2016)

Laffin, John, *The War of Desperation: Lebanon, 1982–85* (London: Osprey, 1985)

Luttwak, Edward & Horowitz, Dan, *The Israeli Army* (London: Allen Lane, 1975)

Matthews, Matt, *We Were Caught Unprepared: The 2006 Hezbollah-Israeli War* (Fort Leavenworth, KS: US Army Combined Arms Center, Combat Studies Institute Press, 2008)

Morris, Benny, *Israel's Border Wars, 1949–1956: Arab Infiltration, Israeli Retaliation, and the Countdown to the Suez War* (Oxford: OUP, 1997)

Rabinovich, Itamar, *The War for Lebanon, 1970–1985* (Ithaca, NY: Cornell University Press, 1985)

Rothenberg, Gunther E., *The Anatomy of the Israeli Army* (London: Batsford, 1979)

Schiff, Ze'ev, *A History of the Israeli Army: 1874 to the Present* (London: Sidgwick & Jackson, 1987)

Schiff, Ze'ev & Ya'ari, Ehud, *Israel's Lebanon War* (New York, NY: Simon & Schuster, 1984)

INDEX

Note: page numbers in bold refer to illustrations, captions and plates. All hardware is Israeli unless otherwise stated.